Bear Tales

Of The Native American Indians

Written and Edited by G.W. Mullins
With Original Art by C.L. Hause

ISBN: 978-1-7377100-7-3

First Edition Printing

Light Of The Moon Publishing has allowed this work to remain exactly as the author intended, verbatim, without editorial input.

Printed in the United States of America

The following book represents a collection of Native American works which are public domain. You may have read the stories before. In true story telling fashion, the stories have been left as close to the original form as possible. In Native American culture, in order to pass the stories along with all information intact, they had to be told pretty much word for word, to keep the legends alive. Many of these stories were translated directly from original Native language texts. With that in mind, please be aware that some spellings and word usage may vary from one tribe to another. For instance, the spelling of "teepee", as used in this book, can also be written as "tipi", and "tepee". All are correct. Also, when using words like "someone", in most native cultures, it would be "some one". So, keep in mind, these are not necessarily misspellings. They are simply dialect and translations.

This book is dedicated to Vince Mullins, my Grandfather (Pawpaw). He was a tall red man with fire in his eyes… who I loved so much.

This book is also dedicated to one of my heroes Chief Dan George, a true visionary.

G.W. Mullins

Chief Dan George, (July 24, 1899 – September 23, 1981) was a chief of the Tsleil-Waututh Nation, a Coast Salish band located on Burrard Inlet in North Vancouver, British Columbia, Canada. He was also an author, poet, actor, and an Officer of the Order of Canada. At the age of 71, he was nominated for an Academy Award for Best Supporting Actor in Little Big Man.

You have noticed that everything as Indian does is in a circle, and that is because the Power of the World always works in circles, and everything tries to be round.... The Sky is round, and I have heard that the earth is round like a ball, and so are all the stars. The wind, in its greatest power, whirls. Birds make their nest in circles, for theirs is the same religion as ours....

~Black Elk, Oglala Sioux Holy Man, 1863-1950

Also Available From G.W. Mullins And C.L. Hause

War Song Tales Of The Native American Indians

Walking With Spirits Native American Myths, Legends, And Folklore
Volumes One Thru Six

The Native American Cookbook

Native American Cooking - An Indian Cookbook With Legends And Folklore

The Native American Story Book - Stories Of The American Indians For Children
Volumes One Thru Five

The Best Native American Stories For Children

Cherokee A Collection of American Indian Legends, Stories And Fables

Creation Myths - Tales Of The Native American Indians

Strange Tales Of The Native American Indians

Spirit Quest - Stories Of The Native American Indians

Animal Tales Of The Native American Indians

Medicine Man - Shamanism, Natural Healing, Remedies And Stories Of The Native American Indians

Native American Legends: Stories Of The Hopi Indians
Volumes One and Two

Totem Animals Of The Native Americans

The Best Native American Myths, Legends And Folklore
Volumes One Thru Three

Ghosts, Spirits And The Afterlife In Native American Indian Mythology And Folklore

The Native American Art Book – Art Inspired By Native American Myths And Legends

Star People, Sky Gods And Other Tales Of The Native American Indians

Animal Tales Of The native American Indians Vol. 2

Origin Tales Of The Native American Indians

THE NATIVE AMERICAN
STORY COLLECTION SERIES
Featuring The Writing Of Best-Selling Author
G.W. MULLINS
And Original Art From
Award Winning Artist
C.L. HAUSE

This is the Earth, healed again, growing green and blue.
I want you to remember this exactly as it is,
and then go and tell the people that if enough of us hold this image in their minds,
we can heal the Earth and make it like it was a long time ago.
- Grandfather Rolling Thunder, Cherokee Medicine Elder

Lakota Instructions for Living

Friend do it this way - that is,
whatever you do in life,
do the very best you can
with both your heart and mind.

And if you do it that way,
the Power Of The Universe
will come to your assistance,
if your heart and mind are in Unity.

When one sits in the Hoop Of The People,
one must be responsible because
All of Creation is related.
And the hurt of one is the hurt of all.
And the honor of one is the honor of all.
And whatever we do affects everything in the universe.

If you do it that way - that is,
if you truly join your heart and mind
as One - whatever you ask for,
that's the Way It's Going To Be.

Passed down from White Buffalo Calf Woman

Table of Contents

Introduction

Native American Mythology began long before the European settlers arrived on North American soil. Contrary to popular beliefs, there is more to Native American Folklore than stories of buffalo hunts, teepee living and animal stories. Hundreds of tribes throughout North American created a huge mythological system that has rivaled that of the Greeks. Many of these tales have been lost, or are often hard to find. This collection represents a history that should be remembered.

As a Native American myself, I embrace these stories. Native Americans tribes offer such a rich heritage. They have recorded a huge amount of their history through storytelling. In these stories you will relive their history and the lives of North America's First People.

The stories in this book have been handed down from generation to generation. And in such tradition, they are now handed down to you, to share with the next generation.

Included in this anthology, are a group of collected works from the well-known, to the often-forgotten tribes. The tales included within this book feature one of the most familiar animals in Native American folklore, the Bear. Often portrayed as powerful and fierce, the Bear was the strong figure in stories, as you will read in the folklore within this collection.

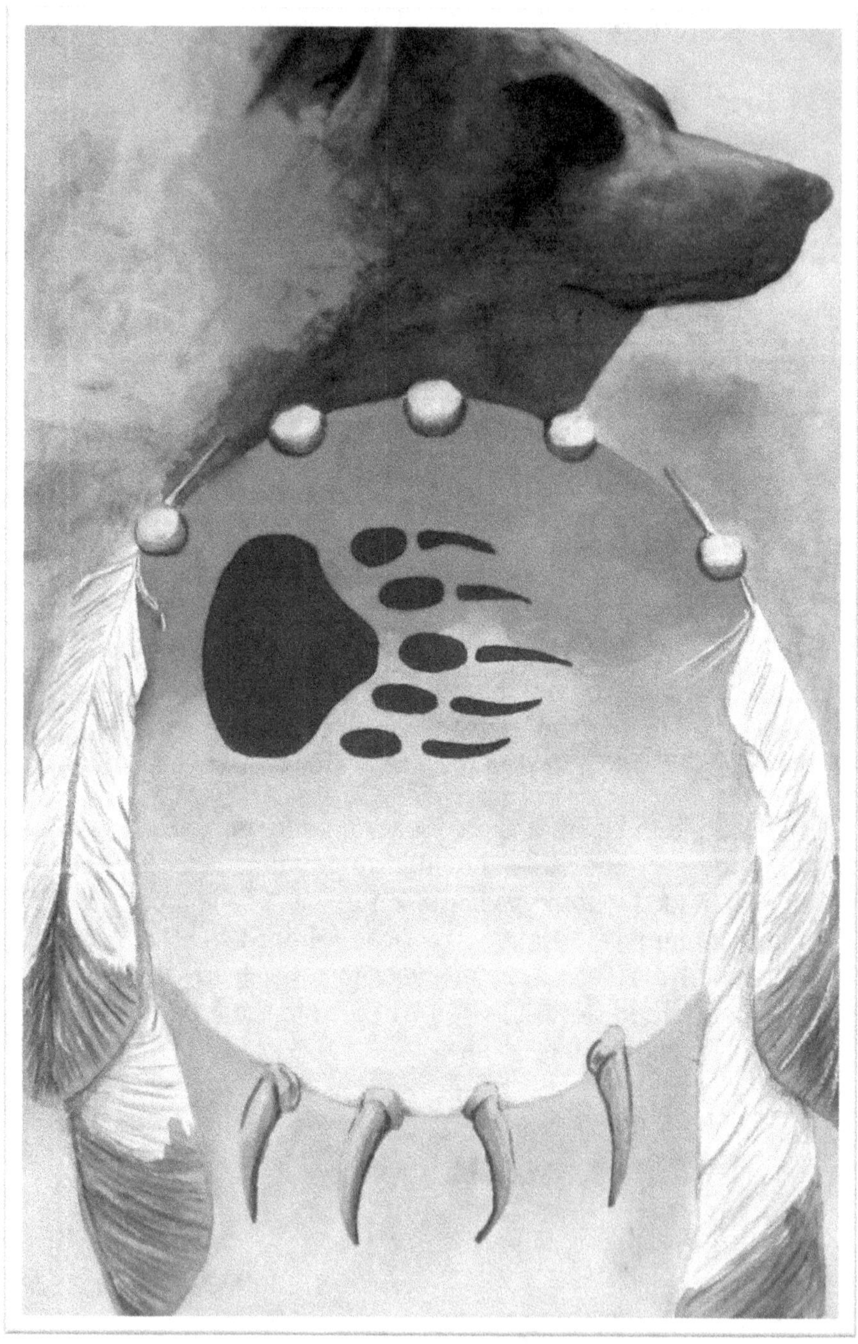

The Woman and her Bear

Eskimo Legend

Long ago in the far north, there lived a village of people known as the Inuit. They lived on the shores of the icy Arctic, and they depended upon the bounty of the salmon and seal and the creatures of the snow to feed themselves. All the young men of the village were hunters and fishermen. One old woman lived alone She had no husband and no sons to hunt or fish for her, and though her neighbors shared their food with her, as was their custom, she was lonely. She longed for a family of her own. She often walked along the shore, looking far out to sea, praying that the gods might send her a son.

One cold winter day, the woman was walking by the sea when she spotted a tiny white polar bear sitting all alone on the thick ice. At once she felt a kinship toward him, for he looked as lonely as she. His mother was nowhere in sight. "Someone must have killed her," she said softly, and she walked onto the ice, picked up the cub and looked into his eyes. "You will be my son," she said. She called him Kunik.

The old woman took her cub back to her home. From that day on, she shared all of her food with Kunik, and a strong bond grew between the two.

The village children loved Kunik, too. Now the woman was never lonely, for her son, the bear, and all the village children kept her company all day. She would stand by her igloo and smile as Kunik and the children rolled in the snow and slid on the ice. Kunik was gentle with the children as if they were his brothers and sisters.

Kunik grew taller and smarter. The children taught him to fish. By springtime he was fishing on his own, and every afternoon he came home carrying fresh salmon for his mother. The old woman was now the happiest of all the villagers. She had plenty of food and a son she loved with all her heart. She was so proud of her little bear that whenever he returned home, she would say proudly to anyone nearby, "He's the finest fisherman in all the village!"

Before long the men began to whisper among themselves. They knew the bear was the most skillful fisherman of the village. They began to feel envious. "What will we do?" they asked each other. "That bear brings home the fattest seals and the biggest salmon." "He must be stopped," one of the men said. "He puts us to shame." They all turned and looked at him. They nodded slowly for although they were envious, they knew how much the old woman loved the bear. "We'll have to kill him. He has grown far too big," one man said. One by one the others agreed, for their envy made them stupid and mean. "Yes" the others said. "He is a danger to our families."

A little boy overheard the men talking. He ran to the old woman's home to tell her of the terrible plan. When the old woman heard the news, she threw her arms around her bear and wept. "No," she said, "they must not kill my child." At once she set off to visit every house in the village. She begged each man not to kill her beautiful bear. "Kill me instead," she wept. "He is my child. I love him dearly."

"He is fat," some of the village men said. "He will make a great feast for the whole village." "He is a danger to our children," the others said. "We cannot let him live."

The old woman saw that the men were determined to kill her son. She rushed home and sat down beside him. "Your life is in danger, Kunik. You must run away. Run away and do not return my child." she wept as she spoke and held him close. "Run away, but do not go so far that I cannot find you," she whispered. And though her heart was breaking, she sent Kunik away. He had tears in his eyes, but he obeyed his mother's wishes.

For many days the old woman and the children grieved their loss. And then one day the old woman rose at dawn and was determined to find Kunik. She walked and walked, calling out his name. After many hours, just as the old woman feared she would never find him, she saw her bear running toward her. He was fat and strong, and his coat was shimmering white. They embraced, and the old woman whispered, "I love you."

But Kunik could see that his mother was hungry, and so he ran to get her fresh meat and fish. With tears in her eyes, the old woman cut up the seal and gave her son the choicest slices of blubber. Promising to return the next day, she set off for home, carrying her meat, her heart filled with joy.

The next day, as she had promised, she went to visit her son. And every day after that, the old woman and her son met, and the bear brought his mother fresh meat and fish.

After a while the villagers grew to understand the love between the woman and the bear was strong and true. And from that point on, they told with pride and respect the tale of the unbroken love between the old woman and her son.

Bear-Woman and Deer-Woman

Lassik Legend Goddard, Journal of American Folk-Lore, xix, 135, No. 2

Grizzly Bear and Doe, the two wives of Chickenhawk, were pounding acorns. When they had finished, one of them said, "Let us go down to the creek and leach the meal."

While they were waiting for the meal to soak, they agreed to hunt one another's heads for lice. Doe looked first in Grizzly's hair. "You have no lice," she said. "Well then," said Grizzly, "I will look in yours." When in her search she reached the Doe's neck she sprinkled in some sand. "You have many lice," she said, "I will chew them." "Ukka! ukka!" cried Doe, "hold on there." Biting her head off, she killed her.

Taking Doe's head and both lots of acorn meal she went back to the house. She put the head in the fire and when the eyes burst with the heat she told the children it was only the white oak log cracking in the fire. "I think it is our mother's head," said one of the Doe's children. "Go a long way off and play," said Grizzly. "You won't be permitted to live long," they heard their mother's head so say to them.

The two bear children and the two fawns went out to play. "Let us play smoke-eachother-out in this hollow log," suggested the fawns. The bears agreed and the fawns went in first. "That's enough, that's enough," they cried. "Now you go in," they told the bears. The fawns fanned the smoke into the log until the bears were smothered.

Going back to the house, one of them held out what she had in her hand and said, "Here is a skunk we killed in a log." "Very well," said the bear mother. Then the other fawn held out hers and said, "Here is a skunk we killed in a log." "Thank you, my niece; after a while I will make a meal upon them," replied Grizzly.

"She is eating her children," she heard some one say. "What did you say?" she asked. "First you killed some one, and now you are eating your own children's hands." She ran after the children who had been taunting her. When she came near them, she called in a pleasant voice, "Well, come home." They ran up on a ridge and barely escaped being caught.

Finally, they came to a place where Crane was fishing by the river. "Grandfather, put your neck across and let us go over on it. An old woman is after us. Put your neck across." They crossed over safely and running to the top of a ridge hid in a hole in a rock. When Grizzly came, Crane put his neck across again for a bridge, but when she was half way over he gave it a sudden twist. She went floating down the middle of the stream.

The Maiden Who Became a Bear

Navaho
The Dîné: Origin Myths of the Navaho Indians Aileen O'Bryan

When the brothers returned that night, they entered the house. Not seeing the Coyote among them, their sister went out to look for him; not finding him she asked her eldest brother what they had done with her husband. The eldest brother said: "We sent him back with the meat a long time ago. We thought that you would have the meat cooked for us by now." The woman looked straight at her brothers and told them that they had killed the Coyote. The brothers said: "No, sister, we have told you the truth. We sent him back with the meat early in the day." But she accused them four times of killing her husband. Four times they gave the same answer. Then she went to the rainbow path and there she found the meat. From there she tracked the Coyote to the canyon's edge and she found where he had been killed by the Swallow People.

After the woman left her brothers to go look for the Coyote the eldest brother said: "Listen now to my words: our sister is about to do something still more evil."

When the woman returned to the house, she told her brothers that the people in the canyon had killed her husband. She would not sit down in the home. She prepared herself to go against the cliff people. First, she took her sewing awls and sharpened them; then she hid her heart and lungs as the Coyote had taught her, and turned herself into a great bear with sharp teeth and claws, and she went forth against the people of the canyon. When she came among them, they shot at her with their arrows, but they did not harm her. When she returned home, she turned back into her woman form. But every night she went out in her bear form and killed the cliff people with her teeth and claws; however, she did not eat them as a wolf or bear would have done.

It was then that the people moved into the caves in the cliff walls. The Rainbow's strength was their strength. The people, in those days, used a rainbow for their ladder as well as for their bridge. They used it and it was not difficult for them to carry up their goods and to build houses in the caves. For a long time, the people abandoned their homes on the floor of the canyon; but the bear woman followed them. She would dig up through the earth and kill them. After that they built their homes of rock in the caves.

Always when she returned to her brothers, she was in her woman form. But her name was now Esdza'shash nadle, the Woman who Became a Bear.

Soon she went out even during the day to kill people. She became so terrible that the Spider People, the Lizard People, and the Swallow People built high in the sides of the canyons where she could not reach them. After a time, the brothers became frightened. They did not know what to do. But they knew that their turn would come; that she would kill them too. The eldest brother had a plan. He, together with the other brothers, pushed the ashes of the fire to one side and they dug a hole under the fireplace. They hid the youngest brother in this hole which had four sides to hold back the earth. They covered the hole with a slab over which they put earth; they then raked the ashes over it and built a fire. Then they went to the east of their dwelling.

When the Bear Woman returned no one was in the house. She went to relieve herself and said: "Whichever way the water runs, that is the direction my brothers have taken." It showed east; so, she followed in her bear form. She tracked them and she killed the 11 brothers. She saw that the youngest was missing. She returned to the house. Again, she went to relieve herself, and she said: "Whichever way it flows there my brother is." But it neither flowed nor fell. So, she went into the house and tore the rocks out. She found her youngest brother under the firestone.

The Bear Woman spoke kind words to him. "Come out, my brother," she said, "your hair looks dirty; it needs washing and dressing; let me care for it." The little breeze whispered in the boy's ear: "She has killed your 11 brothers, and now she wants your life." The little breeze stayed on the boy's ear and told him to have weapons ready when she began to comb his hair. It told him also, to loosen the string ties of his loin cloth. "She will place you facing the sun when she starts to comb your hair; but you must sit so that. you can see her shadow." The woman made her brother sit facing the sun; but be said: "Sister, the sun is too bright for my eyes." After four times she agreed to let him sit where he chose. He sat where he could watch her shadow. She got the grass brush, which they used for the hair, and she brushed his hair oncc or twice; and out grew her lips to the shape of a bear's mouth with long teeth. The boy turned and said: "What is it, sister?" She said: "Oh, I am just sleepy." The breeze was now busy in the boy's ear telling him what would happen and what he should do. He was to be saved; but the price paid was the lives of his 11 brothers.

The boy was told that the fourth time that he caught her changing into the form of a bear he must jump up and run as fast as he could to the place where she had hidden her heart and lungs. "About the moment when she is about to catch you, you will jump over a big cactus. She will have to go around it and you will gain ground. The second time you will jump over a big growth of yucca; the third time, over a log; and the fourth time you will jump over a big boulder."

Now the boy watched her shadow, and each time that he caught her changing into the bear form he turned and looked at her and she became the woman. After the fourth time he had his muscles set, and jumped away from her. Sure enough, she grabbed his belt; but the tie loosened. She was near him when he reached the cactus. He jumped over it; she ran around it. The second time she was near him he jumped over the yucca; the third time he jumped over the fallen log; and the fourth time, over the great boulder. Then her heart became nervous, and the chipmunk who was guarding it screamed. The heart and the lungs were beating up and down just ahead of the boy. They were covered with oak leaves. The Bear Woman cried out: "Oh, brother, brother, stop! There are my heart and my lungs. There is my life."

Now when the boy saw the leaves beating up and down in fright, he jumped over them, and he shot his arrow into them. The Bear Woman fell, and the blood gushed out of her mouth and nostrils. The boy returned near her, and the little breeze told him to stop the blood. It must not flow, for if it met the blood from her heart, she would become whole again. So, the boy pulled the Bear Woman's carcass away. He was angry. He spread her legs and cut out her sex organs. He said: "You have the sex organs of a woman, and great trouble has come of it." He tossed it to the top of a tree and said: "The people of the earth shall use you henceforth." It became the pitch that is found on cedar and pinon trees. Then he cut off her breasts and said: "You have a woman's breasts and still you have caused great trouble."

He tossed them to the top of a tree and said: "The people of the earth shall use you." And they became pinon nuts.

After these things happened many people planned to leave the mesas. They were afraid of the Woman who became a bear. They buried the Calendar Stone; they wrapped their dead; and leaving their belongings, they went away. But before they left, they drew pictures on the rocks of all the things that trouble came from.

Now only the Swallow People and the Lizard, Snake, and Spider People remained. All the others said that they would never return to make the mesa country their home. They moved into Montezuma Valley and built their homes around Ute Mountain. Their main dwellings were Yucca House and a place near a spring east of Ute Mountain. They multiplied and their homes covered quite a lot of territory. They moved to places where they found good water, good building material, and where their plants would grow. But always they came to where their chief person lived. This was a place west of Dolores called Sage Brush Spring. They moved their chief, or head person of their tribe, there. This person was considered sacred, and kept away from the sun and the light all of the time. Where he lived sacred stones were placed at his feet, at his out-stretched arms and head. Prayer sticks guarded his body. Then bluebird feathers were set around him. Whatever he said was done. They lived for a time at Sage Brush Spring; but corn did not grow well there; living was difficult. They moved to the foot of Elk Mountain.

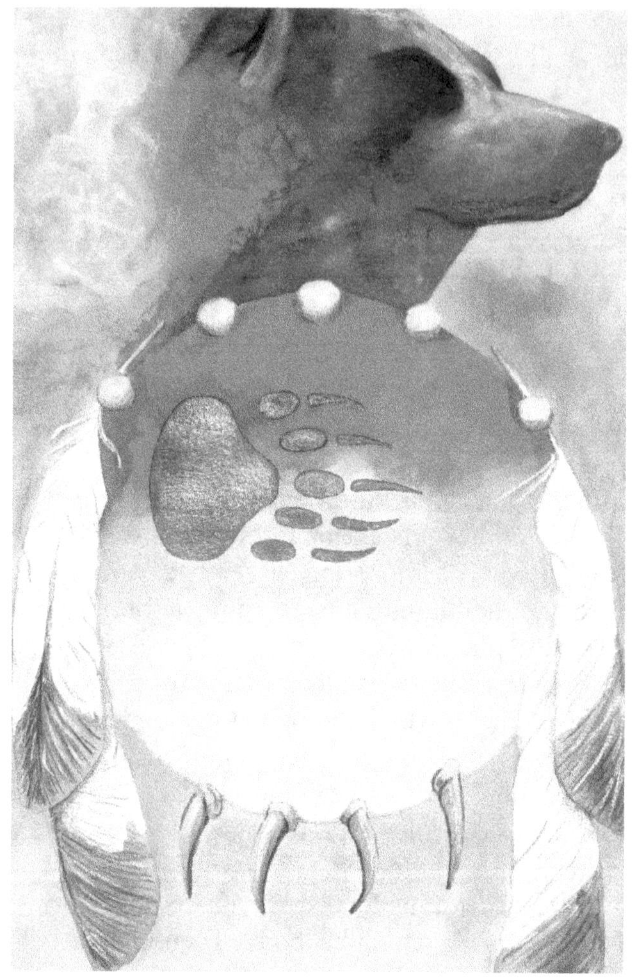

Bear's Lodge

(A story told by the Kiowa People in Wyoming and South Dakota, and by other tribes)

One day long ago a traveling party of the Kiowa People were crossing the great prairie and camped by a stream. Many of the Bear People lived nearby, and they smelled the

Kiowa People. The Bear People were hungry, and some of the bear warriors went out to hunt the Kiowa People.

Seven young girls from the Kiowa camp were out gathering berries, up along the stream, far from the campsite. The Bears came upon them and growled to attack. The girls ran and ran, out across the open prairie, until they came to a large gray rock. They climbed onto the rock, but the bears began to climb the rock also.

The girls began to sing a prayer to the rock, asking it to protect them from the Bear People. No one had ever honored the rock before, and the rock agreed to help them. The rock, who had laid quietly for centuries, began to stand up and reach to the sky. The girls rose higher and higher as the rock stood up. The bear warriors began to sing to the bear gods, and the bears grew taller as the rock rose up.

The bears tried and tried to climb the rock as it grew steeper and higher, but their huge claws only split the rock face into thousands of strips as the rock grew up out of their reach. Pieces of rock were scraped and cut away by the thousands and fell in piles at the foot of the rock. The rock was cut and scarred on all of its sides as the bears fought to climb it.

At last, the bears gave up the hunt, and turned to go back to their own houses. They slowly returned to the original sizes. As the huge bears came back across the prairie, slowly becoming smaller, the Kiowas saw them and broke camp. They fled in fear, and looking back at the towering mountain of rock, they guessed that it must be the lodge of these giant bears. "Tso' Ai'," some people say today, or "Bears' Lodge."

The Kiowa girls were afraid, high up on the rock, and they saw their people break camp and leave them there, thinking the girls had all already been eaten by the bears.

The girls sang again, this time to the stars. The stars were happy to hear their song, and the stars came down and took the seven girls into the sky, the Seven Sisters, and each night they pass over Bears' Lodge and smile in gratitude to the rock spirit.

The Destruction of the Bear

A Jicarilla Apache Legend
Frank Russell, Myths of the Jicarilla Apaches, 1898

An Apache boy, while playing with his comrades, pretended to be a bear, and ran into a hole in the hillside. When he came out his feet and hands had been transformed into bear's paws. A second time he entered the den, and his limbs were changed to the knees and elbows.

Four times he entered the den, and then came forth the voracious cac-tla-yæ that devoured his former fellow-beings. One day the bear met a fox in the mountains. "I am looking for a man to eat," said Bear.

"So am I," said Fox, "but your legs are so big and thick you cannot run very fast to catch them. You ought to allow me to trim down those posts a little, so you can run as swift as I."

Bear consented to have the operation performed, and Fox not only cut the flesh from the legs of Bear, but also broke the bones with his knife, thus killing the dreaded man-eater. Taking the leg bones of Bear with him, he went to the home of the bear family, and there found two other bears.

These monsters preyed upon the people, who were unable to kill them, as they left their hearts at home when off on their marauding expeditions.

Fox remained in hiding until the bears went away. When they ran among the Indians, Fox responded to the cries for assistance, not by flying to attack the bears, but by hastening to cut their hearts in two.

The bears were aware that their hearts had been tampered with, and rushed with all speed to rescue them, but fell dead just before they reached Fox.

Thus, Fox destroyed one of the most dreaded of man's enemies of that primeval time.

O' Great Spirit
help me always
to speak the truth quietly,
to listen with an open mind
when others speak,
and to remember the peace
that may be found in silence.

Cherokee Prayer

They That Chase After the Bear

This version of the legend comes from William Jones' 1907 collection of Mesquakie stories, Fox Texts.

It is said that once on a time long ago in the winter, at the beginning of the season of snow after the first fall of snow, three men went on a hunt for game early on a morning. Upon a hillside into a place where the bush was thick a bear they trailed. One of the men went in following the trail of the bear. And then he started it up running. "Towards the place whence comes the cold is he speeding away!" he said to his companions.

He that headed off on the side which lay towards the source of the cold, "In the direction of the place of the noonday sky is he running!" he said.

Back and forth amongst themselves they kept the bear fleeing. They say that after a while he that was coming up behind chanced to look down at the ground. Behold, green was the surface of the earth lying face up! Now of a truth up into the sky, were they conveyed by the bear! When round about the bush they were chasing it then truly was the time that up into the sky they went. And then he that came up behind cried out to him that was next ahead: "O River-that-joins-Another, let us go back! We are being carried up into the sky!" Thus, said he to River-that-joins-Another. But by him was he not heeded.

Now River-that-joins-Another was he who ran in between the two and a little puppy Hold-Tight he had for a pet.

In the autumn they overtook the bear, and then they slew it. After they had slain it, then boughs of the oak they cut, likewise boughs of the sumac, then laying the bear on top of the leaves they flayed and cut up the bear; after they had flayed and cut it up, then they began slinging and scattering the meat in every direction. Towards the place of the coming of the morning they flung the head; in the winter-time when the morning is about to appear some stars usually rise; it is said that they came from the head of the bear. And also, his backbone, towards the place of the morning they flung it too. They too are commonly seen in the winter-time; they are stars that lie huddled close together; it is said that they came from the backbone.

And they say that these four stars in the lead were the bear, and the three stars at the rear were they who were chasing after the bear. In between two of them is a tiny little star, it hangs near by another; they say that it was the puppy, the pet Hold-Tight of River-that-joins-Another.

Every autumn the oaks and sumacs redden in the leaf because it is then that the hunters lay the bear on top of the leaves and flay and cut it up; then red with blood become the leaves. Such is the reason why every autumn red become the leaves of the oaks and sumacs.

That is the end of the story.

The Hunting of the Great Bear

There were four hunters who were brothers. No hunters were as good as they at following a trail. They never gave up once they began tracking their quarry.

One day, in the moon when the cold nights return, an urgent message came to the village of the four hunters. A great bear, one so large and powerful that many thought it must be some kind of monster, had appeared. The people of the village whose hunting grounds the monster had invaded were afraid. The children no longer went out to play in the woods. The long houses of the village were guarded each night by men with weapons, who stood by the entrances.

Each morning, when the people went outside, they found the huge tracks of the bear in the midst of their village. They knew that soon it would become even bolder.

Picking up their spears and calling to their small dog, the four hunters set forth for that village, which was not far away. As they came closer, they noticed how quiet the woods were. There were no signs of rabbits or deer and even the birds were silent. On a great pine tree they found the scars where the great bear had reared up on hind legs and made deep scratches to mark its territory. The tallest of the brothers tried to touch the highest of the scratch marks with the tip of his spear. "It is as the people feared," the first brother said. "This one we are to hunt is Nyah-gwaheh, a monster bear."

"But what about the magic that the Nyah-gwaheh has?" said the second brother.

The first brother shook his head. "That magic will do it no good if we find its track."

"That's so," said the third brother. "I have always heard that from the old people. Those creatures can only chase a hunter who has not yet found its trail. When you find the track of the Nyah-gwaheh and begin to chase it, then it must run from you."

"Brothers," said the fourth hunter who was the fattest and laziest, "did we bring along enough food to eat? It may take a long time to catch this big bear. I'm feeling hungry."

Before long, the four hunters and their small dog reached the village. It was a sad sight to see. There was no fire burning in the centre of the village and the doors of all the long houses were closed. Grim men stood on guard with clubs and spears and there was no game hung from the racks or skins stretched for tanning. The people looked hungry.

The elder sachem of the village came out and the tallest of the four hunters spoke to him.

"Uncle," the hunter said, "we have come to help you get rid of the monster."

Then the fattest and laziest of the four brothers spoke. "Uncle," he said, "is there some food we can eat? Can we find a place to rest before we start chasing this big bear. I'm tired."

The first hunter shook his head and smiled. "My brother is only joking, Uncle." he said. " We are going now to pick up the monster bear's trail."

"I am not sure you can do that, Nephews," the elder sachem said. "Though we find tracks closer and closer to the doors of our lodges each morning, whenever we try to follow those tracks, they disappear."

The second hunter knelt down and patted the head of their small dog. "Uncle," he said, that is because they do not have a dog such as ours." He pointed to the two black circles above the eyes of the small dog. "Four-Eyes can see any tracks, even those many days old."

"May Creator's protection be with you," said the elder sachem.

"Do not worry. Uncle," said the third hunter, "Once we are on a trail we never stop following until we've finished our hunt," the fourth hunter said. "That's why I think we should have something to eat first." But his brothers did not listen. They nodded to the elder sachem and began to leave. Sighing, the fattest and laziest of the brothers lifted up his long spear and trudged after them.

They walked, following their little dog. It kept lifting up its head, as if to look around with its four eyes. The trail was not easy to find.

"Brothers," the fattest and laziest hunter complained, "don't you think we should rest. We've been walking a long time." But his brothers paid no attention to him. Though they could see no tracks, they could feel the presence of the Nyah-gwaheh. They knew that if they did not soon find its trail, it would make its way behind them. Then they would be the hunted ones.

The fattest and laziest brother took out his pemmican pouch. At least he could eat while they walked along. He opened the pouch and shook out the food he had prepared so carefully by pounding together strips of meat and berries with maple sugar and then drying them in the sun. But instead of pemmican, pale squirming things fell out into his hands. The magic of the Nyah-gwaheh had changed the food into worms.

"Brothers," the fattest and laziest of the hunters shouted, "Let's hurry up and catch that big bear! Look what it did to my pemmican. Now I'm getting angry!"

Meanwhile, like a pale giant shadow, the Nyah-gwaheh was moving through the trees close to the hunters. Its mouth was open as it watched them and its huge teeth shone, its eyes flashed red. Soon it would be behind them and on their trail.

Just then, though, the little dog lifted its head and yelped. "Eh-heh!" the first brother called.

"Four-Eyes has found the trail," shouted the second brother.

"We have the track of the Nyah-gwaheh," said the third brother.

"Big Bear," the fattest and laziest one yelled, "we are after you, now!"

Fear filled the heart of the great bear for the first time and it began to run. As it broke from the cover of the pines, the four hunters saw it, a gigantic white shape, so pale as to appear almost naked. With loud hunting cries, they began to run after it. The great bear's strides were long and it ran more swiftly than a deer. The four hunters and their little dog were swift also though and they did not fall behind. The trail led through the swamps and the thickets. It was easy to read, for the bear pushed everything aside as it ran, even knocking down big trees. On and on they ran, over hills and through valleys. They came to the slope of a mountain and followed the trail higher and higher, every now and then catching a glimpse of their quarry over the next rise. Now though the lazy hunter was getting tired of running. He pretended to fall and twist his ankle.

"Brothers," he called, "I have sprained my ankle. You must carry me."

So his three brothers did as he asked, two of them carrying him by turns while the third hunter carried his spear. They ran more slowly now because of their heavy load, but they were not falling any further behind. The day had turned now into night, yet they could still see the white shape of the great bear ahead of them. They were at the top of the mountain now and the ground beneath them was very dark as they ran across it. The bear was tiring, but so were they. It was not easy to carry their fat and lazy brother. The little dog, Four-Eyes, was close behind the great bear, nipping at its tail as it ran.

"Brothers," said the fattest and laziest one. "Put me down now. I think my leg has gotten better."

The brothers did as he asked. Fresh and rested, the fattest

and laziest one grabbed his spear and dashed ahead of the others. Just as the great bear turned to bite at the little dog, the fattest and laziest hunter leveled his spear and thrust it into the heart of the Nyah-Gwaheh. The monster bear fell dead.

By the time the other brothers caught up, the fattest and laziest hunter had already built a fire and was cutting up the big bear.

"Come on, brothers," he said. "Let's eat. All this running has made me hungry!"

So they cooked the meat of the great bear and its fat sizzled as it dripped from their fire. They ate until even the fattest and laziest one was satisfied and leaned back in contentment. Just then, though, the first hunter looked down at his feet.

"Brothers," he exclaimed, "look below us!"

The four hunters looked down. Below them were thousands of small sparkling lights in the darkness which. They realized, it was all around them.

"We aren't on a mountain top at all," said the third brother. "We are up in the sky." And it was so. The great bear had indeed been magical. Its feet had taken it high above the earth as it tried to escape the four hunters. However, their determination not to give up the chase had carried them up that strange trail.

Just then their little dog yipped twice.

"The great bear!" said the second hunter. "Look!"

The hunters looked. There, where they had piled the bones of their feast the Great Bear was coming back to life and rising to its feet. As they watched, it began to run again, the small dog close on its heels.

"Follow me," shouted the first brother. Grabbing up their spears, the four hunters again began to chase the great bear across the skies.

So it was, the old people say, and so it still is. Each autumn the hunters chase the great bear across the skies and kill it. Then, as they cut it up for their meal, the blood falls down from the heavens and colors the leaves of the maple trees scarlet. They cook the bear and the fat dripping from their fire turns the grass white.

If you look carefully into the skies as the seasons change, you can read that story. The great bear is the square shape some call the bowl of the Big Dipper. The hunters and their small dog (which you can just barely see) are close behind, forming the dipper's handle. When autumn comes and that constellation turns upside down, the old people say. "Ah, the lazy hunter has killed the bear." But as the moons pass and the sky moves once more towards spring, the bear slowly rises back on its feet and the chase begins again.

The Medicine Grizzly Bear

A Pawnee Legend George Bird Grinnell, Published in Harper's monthly magazine, 1901

A long time ago there lived in a camp of Pawnees a certain poor boy. His father had only one pony. Once he had been a leading man in the tribe, but now he seemed to be unlucky.

When he went on the war-path he brought back nothing, and when he fought, he did nothing, and the people did not now look up to him.

There was a chief's son who loved the poor boy, and these two went together all the time. They were like brothers; they used to hunt together and go courting together, and when they were traveling, the poor boy often rode one of the ponies of the chief's son, and the latter used to go to the poor boy's lodge and sleep there with him.

Once the camp went off to hunt buffalo, and the poor boy and the chief's son rode together all the time. After the people had made camp at a certain place, the chiefs decided to stop here for four days, because the buffalo were close by, and they could kill plenty and dry the meat here. North of the camp was a hill on which grew many cedar-trees, and during the day the poor boy had overheard people saying that many Indians had been killed on that hill, among those trees. They said that no one ought to go there, for it was a dangerous place.

That night the chief's son went over to his friend's lodge to sleep there, but before they went to bed he left the lodge for a time, and while he was gone the poor boy, as he sat there waiting, began to think about himself and how unhappy he was. He remembered how poor he and his father were, and how everybody looked down on them and despised them, and it did not seem to him that things would ever be any better for them than they were now. For a long time he sat there thinking about all these things, and the more he thought of them the worse they seemed, and at last he felt that he was no longer glad to live, and he made up his mind to go up into those cedars.

He went out of the lodge and started to go up toward the trees. It was bright moonlight, so that he could see well. Just before he reached the edge of the timber he crossed a ravine, and saw there many skeletons of people who had been killed. The ground was white with these bones. He went on into the cedars, and came to a ravine leading up the hills, and followed it. As he went on he saw before him a trail and followed it, and when he came to the head of the ravine there was a big hole in the bank, and the trail led to it. He stopped for a moment when he came to his hole, but then he went in, and when he had entered he saw there, sitting by the fire, a big she-bear and some little cubs.

As the boy stood there looking at her, the she-bear said to him: "I am sorry that you have come here. My husband is the one who kills persons and brings them here for the children and me to eat. You had better go back to your people quickly, or he will eat you up. He has gone hunting, but he will soon be back again. If he finds you here, he will kill you."

The poor boy said: "Well, I came here on purpose to be killed, and I give myself up to you. I shall be glad to be eaten by you. I am here ready to be killed. I am yours. Take me."

The she-bear said: "Oh, I wish I could do something to save you, but I cannot. He is one of those bad bears -- a grizzly -- medicine. I can do nothing for you, but I will try. As soon as you hear any noise outside -- any one coming -- pick up that cub, the littlest one, and hold it in your arms. When he comes in he will tell you to put it down, but do not do so. Hold it tight; he loves that one best of all."

All at once the boy heard outside the cave the noise of a bear snorting and grunting. The she-bear said, "Pick up the cub, quick; he is coming." The boy caught up the little bear, and held it tight to his breast. All at once the noise came to the mouth of the den and stopped. It was the Bear. The boy could hear him talking. He said: "Here! somebody has been about my house. I smell human beings. Yes, he even came in. Where is he? Let me see him, so that I may jump upon him and kill him."

When he came in he saw the boy, and seemed very angry. He stood up on his hind feet and threw up his hands, and then came down again and struck his paws on the ground, and then rose up and snorted "whoof," and blew out red dust from his nostrils, and then came down and jumped about, and sometimes sprang toward the boy, as though he were going to seize him. He was very terrible, and the boy was very much afraid.

The Bear called out to the boy in a loud voice: "How dare you take up my child and hold it? Let it go, or I will tear you to pieces and eat you." But the boy still held the cub. No matter what the Bear said or what he did, the boy held fast to the cub.

When the Bear saw that the boy would not let the cub go, he became quiet, and no longer seemed angry. He said: "Boy, you are my son. Put down your brother, for now he is your brother. He shall go with you, he shall be your companion, and shall be with you always as your guide and helper. He has told me your story, and how you are poor, unhappy, and now he has kept you from being eaten up. I have taken pity on you, and we will send you back to your people, where you may do some good among them. My son, I am at the head of all these animal lodges, down at Pahuk and at Pahur and everywhere else. I am at the head; there is no animal living that is stronger than I; none that I cannot kill. If a man shoots at me, I make the arrow to fall from my skin without hurting me. Look up around my lodge. See these arrows, these guns, these leggings, these beads, and the medicine that men have brought, thinking to kill me; but I have killed them, and have taken these things, and keep them here."

"I knew that your people were coming to this place to hunt. I drove the buffalo over, so that the people should stop here and hunt and kill meat, in order that you might come to my lodge. I know all your feelings. I know that you are sorry for your poor father, my brother, and I wished you to come here, so that I might make you my son and give my power to you, so that you may become a great man among your people. I know that they are now killing buffalo, and that they will be camped here for four days."

"Now, my son, set your brother free. All the power that I have I give to you. I shall kill my son, your little brother there, and give you his skin to keep and to carry away with you, so that he may be your companion and may be with you always. Your brother, your friend at the camp, is looking for you, mourning for you, for he thinks you dead, but tomorrow night you shall see him, and shall tell him to rejoice for you and not to mourn. You shall tell him where you have been."

The little bear that he was holding said to the boy: "It is all right now, brother; put me down. My father means what he says. I am glad that I am going to be with you, my brother." The boy put him down.

Then the Bear said to his wife: "Get up. Take that gun." The she-bear took the gun, and they walked around the fire-place in a circle, and sang, and the boy looked on. The Bear took the gun and told the boy to look at them, and to watch carefully everything that they did. After a little he stopped, and shot his wife, and she fell down dead. Then he put down the gun, and went to the she-bear and put his mouth on the wound, and breathed on it and snorted "woof," and sucked in his breath and took the bullet out, and went around the lodge, singing and making motions, and then he took hold of the she-bear and lifted her to her feet, and supported her, and pushed her around, and helped her, and at last she walked, and was well. Then he called the boy to him and said, "Now I will do the same thing to you." And he did the same thing to the boy, and brought him to life in the same way. Then he said, "That is one power I give you to-night."

Then he gave the gun to the boy and went to the other side of the lodge, and sat up, and said, "Now I will open my mouth, and you shoot me right in the mouth." He opened his mouth, and the boy shot him, and he fell over. After a moment he got up on his feet and slapped his paws on his chest several times, and the bullet came out of his mouth, and he walked around the fireplace two or three times, and made motions and grunted, and then he was well. Then he took the boy in his arms, and hugged him and kissed him and breathed on him, and said: "Now I give you my power. Go over there and I will shoot you as you shot me. Do just as I did." The boy went over there, and the Bear shot him, and the boy did just as the Bear had done, and made himself well.

The Bear then put an arrow in the gun and shot it at the boy, and when the smoke cleared away the boy found the arrow fast in his throat, the feather end sticking out. The Bear took it out and made him well, and gave him also this power.

Then the Bear told him to load the gun with a ball and to shoot it at him, and he did so, and shot the Bear, but the lead was made flat and dropped to the ground. The bullet did not go into the Bear.

The Bear now told the boy to take the bow and arrow and to shoot at him with all his strength. The boy did this, but the arrow did not go through the Bear, but the spike rolled up and the shaft was split. The Bear said: "Now you see, my son, that the gun and the bow, the bullet and the arrow, cannot harm me. You shall have the same power. When you go into battle you shall not carry a gun nor arrows, for they are not mine, but you shall take this paint and put it all over your body, then put this feather on your head, and take this club, which is part of my jawbone. All these things have my power and medicine. When you are carrying these things your enemy cannot hurt you, even if you run right on to him; but with one stroke of this club, you shall kill your enemy.

The next morning the Bear took the boy out on the prairie and showed him the different roots and leaves of medicines, and told him how to use them; how he should eat some medicine and then he could cure the wounded by just breathing on the wound.

That night the Bear said to him: "Hereafter you shall have the same feelings as the bear. When you get angry, you will have a grunt like a bear; and if you get too fierce, teeth like a bear's will stick out of your mouth, so that the people will know that you are very angry. You shall have my power, and you can go into any of the lodges of the animals, of which I am the chief." And he told him how to get into these lodges.

That day they stayed in the Bear's lodge, and the Bear took the claw off from his little finger and gave it and a little bundle of medicine to the boy. He said, "Take this claw and this bundle of medicine and put them on a string and wear them on your neck always, the claw hanging in front." He taught him how to make plums grow on trees, and how to make ground-cherries come out of his mouth.

That night he sent the boy back to the camp. He said: "Tell your father and mother not to mourn for you, for you will return in two days more. I have driven plenty of buffalo to this place, and they will kill them and dry the meat. Now go to the camp and get a pipe and some tobacco, and bring them here."

The boy went back to the camp. When he went into the lodge his father and mother were glad to see him. He told them not to be anxious about him, and not to say anything about his having been away. Then he went out and found his brother, the chief's son, asleep. He said to him: "Wake up, brother. I want you to get some tobacco and a pipe from your father. Tell no one that it is for me. Bring it here. I want to smoke with you. I am going away again, but you must stay in camp. I will be back in a few days." The chief's son got the things and gave them to the boy. He wanted to go with him, but the poor boy would not let him.

That same night the boy went back to the Bear's den, carrying with him the pipe and tobacco. After he went into the lodge he filled his pipe and lighted it, and he and the Bear smoked together. The Bear said to him: "After you have gone home, whenever you smoke, always point your pipe toward my den and ask me to smoke with you. After lighting your pipe, point it first to Atius Tirawat, and then blow a few whiffs to me. Then I shall know that you still remember me. All my power comes from Atius. He made me. There will be an end to my days as there is to those of every mortal. So long as I live I shall protect you; when I die of old age, you shall die too."

After this he said, "Now bring my youngest boy here." The boy brought the little cub, and the Bear said, "Now kill him." The boy hesitated to do this. He did not want to kill the little bear, but it said to him: "Go on, my brother, kill me. After this I am going to be a spirit, and always to be with you." Then the boy killed him, and skinned him, and tanned his hide. After it was tanned he put some red medicine paint on the hide. When this was done the Bear told him to put his paint, his feathers, and his war-club in this hide, and to wrap them up and make a bundle of them.

Then he said: "Now, my son, go to your people, and when you get home hang your bundle up at the back of the lodge, and let the people know nothing of all this. Keep it secret. Wherever you go, or wherever you are, I shall be with you."

The boy went home to the camp, and told his mother to hang up his bundle, as the Bear had said. Next morning, he was in camp and all the people saw him. They were surprised, for they had thought that he had been killed. By this time the Pawnees had all the buffalo they wanted, and the next day they started back to their village.

After they had reached their home, the boy told the chief's son that he wanted him to go off with him on the war-path. His brother said: "It is good. I will go." The poor boy took his bundle, and they started. After traveling many days, they came to a camp of the enemy. They went into the village in the daytime, and took many horses and started away with them, riding hard. Soon the enemy pursued them, and at length they could see them coming, and it seemed as if they must soon overtake them. Then the poor boy got off his horse and stopped, telling his brother to go on, driving the horses.

The boy had painted himself red over his whole body. He held his war-club in his hand, and had his feather tied on his head and the little bear-skin on his back. The enemy soon came up and tried to kill him, but they could not. He would run after one and kill him, and all the others would shoot at him with their arrows, but they could not hurt him, and at last they left him and went back, and he went on and overtook the chief's son. Then his brother saw that he had great power.

After this they traveled on slowly, and at last reached the village. His brother told the people that this man was powerful, that they had taken the horses in broad daylight, and the young man had stayed behind on foot and fought the enemy off, while he drove on the horses.

A few days after they reached home a war-party of the enemy attacked the village. All the Pawnees went out to fight them, but the poor boy stayed behind in the lodge. He took down his bundle, filled the pipe, and pointed it first to Atius, and then toward the Bear's lodge, and smoked. Then he took the paint and mixed it with grease, and rubbed it all over his body except his face: that he painted black.

Then he put the feather on his head and the little bear-robe on his back, and took his war-club in his hand and started out. The Bear had told him that in going into battle he must never start toward the east, but must attack going toward the west. So, he went around, and came on the battle-field from one side.

As he came up, he saw that his people were having a hard time, and were being driven back. There was one of the enemy, who seemed to be the bravest of all. The poor boy rushed at this man and killed him with his club, and then ran back to his own line. When his people looked at him, and saw that it was really the poor boy who had just done so brave a deed, they knew that what the chief's son had said was true. When he started again to rush toward the enemy's line, all the Pawnees followed him.

He ran among the enemy, and with his club killed one here and one there, and the enemy became afraid and ran, and the Pawnees followed and killed many of them. That night they returned to the village, rejoicing over the victory. Everybody was praising the young man. Old men were calling his name, young women were singing about him, and old women dancing before him. People no longer made fun of his father or mother, or of him. Now they looked upon him as a great and powerful person.

The Bear had told him that when he wanted his name

changed, he must call himself Ku ruks la war uks ti, Medicine Bear.

That night the Bear came to the boy in his sleep and spoke to him. He said: "My son, tomorrow the chief of the tribe is going to ask you to take his daughter for your wife, but you must not do this yet. I wish you to wait until you have done certain things. If you take a wife before that time, your power will go from you."

The next day the chief came to Medicine Bear and asked him to marry his daughter, and told him the people wanted him to be their head chief. He refused.

Some time after this all the different tribes that had been attacked by him joined forces and came down together to fight the Pawnees. All the people went out to meet them, but he stayed in his lodge and painted himself, and put his feather in his head and the bear-claw on his neck and his bear-skin on his back, and smoked as he always did, and took his club and went out. When he came to the battle, the Pawnees were having a hard time, because the enemy were so many.

Medicine Bear charged, and killed a man, and then came back, and the second time he charged the people charged all together, following him, and they killed many and drove the enemy off, and those who had the fastest horses were the only ones who got away. The Pawnees went home to the village.

Everybody rejoiced, and there were many scalp-dances. Now the poor boy was more highly thought of than ever. Even the chiefs bowed their heads when they saw him. They could not equal him. This time he called himself Ku ruks ti carish, Angry Bear.

After the excitement had quieted down, one day the head chief said: "Medicine Bear, in all this tribe there is no chief who is equal to you. Sit down by my daughter. Take her for your wife, and take my place as chief. I and my wife will go out of this lodge, and it shall be yours. You shall be the chief of the tribe. Whatever you say we will abide by." The poor boy said: "My father, I will think about this.

By morning I will let you know." In the night, before he slept, he filled the pipe and smoked as the Bear had told him to do, and then he went to bed. In dreams the Bear said to him: "My son, you have done what I wished you to do. Now the power will remain with you as long as you shall live. Now you can marry, if you will."

But the boy was not yet ready to do this. The girl was very pretty, and he liked her, but he felt that before he married there were still some things that he must do. He called his brother and said to him, "Go, kill the fattest of the buffalo; bring it to me, and I will take a long journey with you." His brother went hunting and killed a buffalo, and brought the meat home, and they dried it and made a bundle of it. Medicine Bear told his brother to carry this bundle and a rawhide rope and a little hatchet, and they started on a journey toward the Missouri River. One day toward evening they reached the river, and they found themselves on top of a steep-cut bluff. The river ran at its foot. The poor boy cut a cottonwood pole and drove it into the ground, and tied the rope to it, and then tied the other end of the rope about his brother's body.

Then he sharpened a stick and gave it to his brother and said: "Now take the bundle of meat, and I will let you down over the bank. You must put the meat on a ledge of the cliff, and when the birds come you must feed them. Give a piece to the first one that comes, and then take your sharp stick and get another piece, and so feed all the birds. They are the ones that have power, and they can take pity on you." So he let the chief's son down.

The first bird that came was a buzzard, then an eagle, then hawks and owls, all kinds of birds that kill their prey. He fed them all. While he was doing this, the poor boy was above lying on top of the bank. Late in the afternoon, just as the sun was going down, he saw, far up the river, what looked like a flock of geese coming. They came nearer and nearer, and at last passed out of sight under the bank.

Afterward, when he looked down on the river, he could see in the water red light as if it were all on fire, and as he lay on the bank, he could hear down below him the sound of drumming and singing just as plain as could be, and all the time the chief's son was hanging there in front of the bank, and the poor boy would call down to him to cry and ask the animals to take pity on him. When Medicine Bear had done this, he started back and went home, leaving the chief's son hanging there.

The chief's son staid there all the night and all the next day, and for three days and nights, and on the night of the fourth day he fell asleep. When he awoke he was in a lodge. It was under the Missouri River. When he looked about him, he saw that those in the lodge were all animals. There was the beaver, there was the otter, two buffalo, the antelope, hawks, owls, ermines, bears, frogs, woodpeckers, catfish -- all kinds of animals. On each side of the lodge was a little pool, and in each pool sat a goose, and every time they sang, the geese would shake their wings on the water, and it sounded just like drumming.

The chief of the animals spoke to him, saying: "My son, at this time we can do nothing for you. We must first send our messenger up to the Bear's lodge to ask him what we may do for you." While he was saying this the Bear's servant entered the lodge and said: "My father, it is all right. Our father the Bear told me to say to you that his son has sent this young man to you, and you must exert all your power for him."

Now the animals began to make ready to use their power to help the chief's son. First the Beaver talked to the young man, to tell him of his powers and his ways, so that he might perform wonderful acts. How he should take the branch of a tree and strike a man with its point and it would go through him, and then how to draw it out and to make the man well again. He gave him the power to do this. He taught him how to take a stick two feet long and swallow it, and then take it out again from his throat, and gave him this power.

The Otter gave him the power, if his enemies ever attacked him, to break their arrows with his teeth and shoot back the shaft without a spike, and if he hit an enemy with the shaft, it would kill him. "The poison from your mouth will kill him," he said.

The Ground-dog said: "My son, here is my little one. I give him to you. Take him, and if you have an enemy among the doctors in your tribe, take this little one down to the water early in the morning and dip his nose in the water, and when you take it out it will have a piece of liver in its mouth. The man who has tried to kill you will be found dead."

The Owl said: "My son, I give you power to see in the night. When you go on the warpath and want to take horses, the night will be like daytime for you."
The Hawk said: "My son, I give you power to run swiftly,

and I give you my war-club, which is my wing. You shall strike your enemy with it only once, and the blow shall kill him. Take also this little black rope; you shall use it when you go on the war-path to catch horses. Take also this scalp which you see hanging down from my claw. You shall be a great man for scalping."

Each of the other animals gave him all his kinds of power.

For two days and two nights, they taught him the different kinds of power, and for two days and two nights they taught him the different kinds of roots and herbs for healing the sick. They said to him: "You shall be the great doctor of your people. Every now and then you must bring us tobacco, so that we can smoke."

They further told him that at this time they could teach him only a little, but that afterward, one at a time, they would meet him out on the prairie, and would teach him more. At last they said: "Now it is time for you to go. Your friend has come, and is waiting for you out on the prairie."

The Buffalo now stood up and said: "My son, I want to be with you always. I give you my robe. Wear it wherever you go, that the people may know that you come from this place." All the animals said, "We want to be with you too." Each one of the birds took off a feather and put it on the robe, and each animal put one of its claws on it, and some put medicine on it. In one of the holes the Beaver tied a little sweet-grass, and others did the same. By the time they were through, the robe was all covered with feathers and claws and smelt sweet. The animals had put their medicine on it so that it smelt sweet. Then the animals said, "Go, my son, to your people, and bring us something to smoke, so that we may be satisfied."

Presently the chief's son found himself upon the bluff, facing his brother. His brother grasped him in his arms and said: "Oh, my brother, you smell nice. What a fine robe you have on! Look at all these feathers." They hugged each other. Then they went home together. The chief's son had a bundle that the animals had given him.

Soon after this the Pawnees had a big doctors' dance. These boys went into the doctors' lodge and said: "Doctors, you are the head doctors, but we have come to-night to visit you. We want to do a few things ourselves." The doctors all said "Lau-a." The young men took seats close to the door, which is the most important place in this dance. All the doctors were surprised, and said "Uh!"

The Bear boy got up first and began shooting at the chief's son, just as he had done with the Bear, and all the doctors thought he was powerful, shooting at this young man and curing him. When he got through, it was the other boy's turn. He would take a long sharp stick and thrust it through his brother, and then heal him again, and then take a knife and stab him, and then cure him. He did some powerful things, more so than his brother had done. After the doctors had seen all these things, they all said, "Let us have these two for our head doctors." But the poor boy said: "Not so. This one who is sitting by me has more power than I have. He ought to be the head doctor, for I am a warrior, and can never stay in the camp to doctor people. My brother has gone into the animals' lodge, and they have given him more power than I possess." So the chief's son was chosen to be the head doctor.

When the doctors' dance was over, the two brothers at once started to go to the animals' lodge, carrying with them tobacco and a pipe. When they got there, the chief's son told his brother to wait on the bank, that he was going down to take the tobacco and the pipe to his fathers.

He jumped off the steep bank into the river, down into the door of the lodge, and went in. When they saw him all the animals slapped their mouths and called out. They were glad to see him. After smoking with them, he went back to his friend. After that the chief's son would go off by himself and would meet the animals on the hills. They would tell him about different roots, and how to doctor this disease and that. He would come back with some roots and herbs and put them away.

Finally, the head chief sent for the Bear man and said to him: "My son, I offered you my lodge, my daughter, and the whole tribe. Now take all this. Let me go out of this lodge and look for another one, and you stay here with my daughter." The young man said: "What of my brother? Send for the other chief. Let him give his daughter, his lodge, his people, to him, and this day we will accept your gifts to us. My brother will after this be the head doctor of this tribe." The other chief when asked to do this agreed, and it was so done.

The Bear man went often on the warpath, but his brother stayed at home, and fought against the enemy only when they attacked the village. He took charge of the doctors' lodge. The Bear man after this had some children, and when they had grown up he told his son the secrets of his power. He was now beginning to grow old, and his son went on the warpath, while he stayed at home.

One night he had a dream about his father the Bear. The Bear said to him: "My son, I made you great and powerful among your people. The hairs of my body are falling and soon I shall die. Then you too will die. Tell your son all the secret powers that I gave you. He shall keep the same power that you have had."

Soon after this the old Bear must have died, for the man died. Before he died he said to his brother: "Do not mourn for me, for I shall always be near you. Take care of your people. Cure them when they are sick, and always be their chief."

When the enemy came and attacked these people and wounded any, the chief's son was always there and always cured them. He was a great doctor. At last he also died, but his son had the same kind of power. But these two sons never had so great a power as their fathers.

The Badger and the Bear

Lakota Legend

On the edge of a forest there lived a large family of badgers. In the ground their dwelling was made. Its walls and roof were covered with rocks and straw. Old father badger was a great hunter. He knew well how to track the deer and buffalo.

Every day he came home carrying on his back some wild game. This kept mother badger very busy, and the baby badgers very chubby. While the well-fed children played about, digging little make-believe dwellings, their mother hung thin sliced meats upon long willow racks. As fast as the meats were dried and seasoned by sun and wind, she packed them carefully away in a large thick bag.

This bag was like a huge stiff envelope, but far more beautiful to see, for it was painted all over with many bright colors. These firmly tied bags of dried meat were laid upon the rocks in the walls of the dwelling. In this way they were both useful and decorative. One day father badger did not go off for a hunt. He stayed at home, making new arrows. His children sat about him on the ground floor.

Their small black eyes danced with delight as they watched the gay colors painted upon the arrows. All of a sudden there was heard a heavy footfall near the entrance way. The oval-shaped door-frame was pushed aside. In stepped a large black foot with great big claws. Then the other clumsy foot came next. All the while the baby badgers stared hard at the unexpected comer. After the second foot, in peeped the head of a big black bear!

His black nose was dry and parched. Silently he entered the dwelling and sat down on the ground by the doorway. His black eyes never left the painted bags on the rocky walls. He guessed what was in them. He was a very hungry bear. Seeing the racks of red meat hanging in the yard, he had come to visit the badger family.

Though he was a stranger and his strong paws and jaws frightened the small badgers, the father said, "Hau, how, friend! Your lips and nose look feverish and hungry. Will you eat with us?"

"Yes, my friend," said the bear. "I am starved. I saw your racks of red fresh meat, and knowing your heart is kind, I came hither. Give me meat to eat, my friend."

Hereupon the mother badger took long strides across the room, and as she had to pass in front of the strange visitor, she said: "Ah han! Allow me to pass!" which was an apology.

"Hau, hau!" replied the bear, drawing himself closer to the wall and crossing his shins together.

Mother badger chose the most tender red meat, and soon over a bed of coals she broiled the venison.

That day the bear had all he could eat. At nightfall he rose, and smacking his lips together (that is the noisy way of saying "the food was very good!") he left the badger dwelling. The baby badgers, peeping through the door-flap after the shaggy bear, saw him disappear into the woods near-by.

Day after day the crackling of twigs in the forest told of heavy footsteps. Out would come the shame black bear. He never lifted the door-flap, but thrusting it aside entered slowly in. Always in the same place by the entrance way he sat down with crossed shins. His daily visits were so regular that mother badger placed a fur rug in his place. She did not wish a guest in her dwelling to sit upon the bare hard ground.

At last, one time when the bear returned, his nose was bright and black. His coat was glossy. He had grown fat upon the badger's hospitality. As he entered the dwelling a pair of wicked gleams shot out of his shaggy head.

Surprised by the strange behavior of the guest who remained standing upon the rug, leaning his round back against the wall, father badger queried, "Hau, my friend! What?"

The bear took one stride forward and shook his paw in the badger's face. He said: "I am strong, very strong!"

"Yes, yes, so you are," replied the badger. From the farther end of the room mother badger muttered over her bead work: "Yes, you grew strong from our well-filled bowls."

The bear smiled, showing a row of large sharp teeth. "I have no dwelling. I have no bags of dried meat. I have no arrows. All these I have found here on this spot," said he, stamping his heavy foot. "I want them! See! I am strong!" repeated he, lifting both his terrible paws.

Quietly the father badger spoke, "I fed you. I called you friend, though you came here a stranger and a beggar. For the sake of my little ones leave us in peace."

Mother badger, in her excited way, had pierced hard through the buckskin and stuck her fingers repeatedly with her sharp awl until she had laid aside her work. Now, while her husband was talking to the bear, she motioned with her hands to the children. On tiptoe they hastened to her side.

For reply came a low growl. It grew louder and more fierce. "Wa-ough!" he roared, and by force hurled the badgers out. First the father badger; then the mother. The little badgers he tossed by pairs. He threw them hard upon the ground.

Standing in the entranceway and showing his ugly teeth, he snarled, "Be gone!" The father and mother badger, having gained their feet, picked up their kicking little babes, and, wailing aloud, drew the air into their flattened lungs till they could stand alone upon their feet. No sooner had the baby badgers caught their breath than they howled and shrieked with pain and fright. Ah! what a dismal cry was theirs as the whole badger family went forth wailing from out their own dwelling!

A little distance away from their stolen house the father badger built a small round hut. He made it of bent willows and covered it with dry grass and twigs. This was shelter for the night; but alas! it was empty of food and arrows. All day father badger prowled through the forest, but without his arrows he could not get food for his children. Upon his return, the cry of the little ones for meat, the shad quiet of the mother with bowed head, hurt him like a poisoned arrow wound. "I'll beg meat for you!" said he in an unsteady voice.

Covering his head and entire body in a long loose robe he halted beside the big black bear. The bear was slicing red meat to hang upon the rack. He did not pause for a look at the comer. As the badger stood there unrecognized, he saw that the bear had brought with him his whole family. Little cubs played under the high-hanging new meats. They laughed and pointed with their wee noses upward at the thin sliced meats upon the poles.

"Have you no heart, Black Bear? My children are starving. Give me a small piece of meat for them," begged the badger.

"Wa-ough!" growled the angry bear, and pounced upon the badger. "Be gone!" said he, and with his big hind foot he sent father badger sprawling on the ground. All the little ruffian bears hooted and shouted "ha-ha!" to see the beggar fall upon his face.

There was one, however, who did not even smile. He was the youngest cub. His fur coat was not as black and glossy as those his elders wore. The hair was dry and dingy. It looked much more like kinky wool. He was the ugly cub.

Poor little baby bear! He had always been laughed at by his older brothers. He could not help being himself. He could not change the differences between himself and his brothers. Thus again, though the rest laughed aloud at the badger's fall, he did not see the joke. His face was long and earnest. In his heart he was shad to see the badgers crying and starving. In his breast spread a burning desire to share his food with them. "I shall not ask my father for meat to give away. He would say 'No!' Then my brothers would laugh at me," said the ugly baby bear to himself.

In an instant, as if his good intention had passed from him, he was singing happily and skipping around his father at work. Singing in his small high voice and dragging his feet in long strides after him, as if a prankish spirit oozed out from his heels, he strayed off through the tall grass. He was ambling toward the small round hut.

When directly in front of the entranceway, he made a quick side kick with his left hind leg. Lo! there fell into the badger's hut a piece of fresh meat. It was tough meat, full of sinews, yet it was the only piece he could take without his father's notice. Thus having given meat to the hungry badgers, the ugly baby bear ran quickly away to his father again.

On the following day the father badger came back once more. He stood watching the big bear cutting thin slices of meat. "Give..." he began, when the bear turning upon him with a growl, thrust him cruelly aside.

The badger fell on his hands. He fell where the grass was wet with the blood of the newly carved buffalo. His keen starving eyes caught sight of a little red clot lying bright upon the green. Looking fearfully toward the bear and seeing his head was turned away, he snatched up the small thick blood.

Underneath his girdled blanket he hid it in his hand. On his return to his family, he said within himself: "I'll pray the Great Spirit to bless it."

Thus he built a small round lodge. Sprinkling water upon the heated heap of sacred stones within, he made ready to purge his body. "The buffalo blood, too, must be purified before I ask a blessing upon it," thought the badger.

He carried it into the sacred vapor lodge. After placing it near the sacred stones, he sat down beside it. After a long silence, he muttered: "Great Spirit, bless this little buffalo blood." Then he arose, and with a quiet dignity stepped out of the lodge.

Close behind him some one followed. The badger turned to look over his shoulder and to his great joy he beheld a Lakota brave in handsome buckskins. In his hand he carried a magic arrow. Across his back dangled a long fringed quiver.

In answer to the badger's prayer, the avenger had sprung from out the red globules.

"My son!" exclaimed the badger with extended right hand.

"Hau, father," replied the brave; "I am your avenger!"

Immediately the badger told the sad story of his hungry little ones and the stingy bear. Listening closely the young man stood looking steadily upon the ground. At length the father badger moved away. "Where?" queried the avenger.

"My son, we have no food. I am going again to beg for meat," answered the badger.

"Then I go with you," replied the young brave. This made the old badger happy. He was proud of his son. He was delighted to be called "father" by the first human creature.

The bear saw the badger coming in the distance. He narrowed his eyes at the tall stranger walking beside him. He spied the arrow. At once he guessed it was the avenger of whom he had heard long, long ago.

As they approached, the bear stood erect with a hand on his thigh. He smiled upon them. "How, badger, my friend! Here is my knife. Cut your favorite pieces from the deer," said he, holding out a long thin blade.

"Hau!" said the badger eagerly. He wondered what had inspired the big bear to such a generous deed.

The young avenger waited till the badger took the long knife in his hand. Gazing full into the black bear's face, he said: "I come to do justice. You have returned only a knife to my poor father. Now return to him his dwelling."

His voice was deep and powerful. In his black eyes burned a steady fire. The long strong teeth of the bear rattled against each other, and his shaggy body shook with fear.

"Ahow!" cried he, as if he had been shot. Running into the dwelling he gasped, breathless and trembling, "Come out, all of you! This is the badger's dwelling. We must flee to the forest for fear of the avenger who carries the magic arrow."

Out they hurried, all the bears, and disappeared into the woods. Singing and laughing, the badgers returned to their own dwelling.

Then the avenger left them. "I go," said he in parting, "over the Earth."

The White Faced Bear

Aleut Legend

In a tribal village there lived a mighty bear-hunter. For more than three years, he had been constantly successful in killing so many that his friend tried to persuade him to stop hunting.

"If you insist upon hunting one more bear, you will come across a huge bear who might kill you," he said. The hunter ignored his friend's advice and replied, "I will attack every bear I come across."

A few days later the hunter started out and saw a bear with two cubs. He decided this was not the huge bear he had been worried about, so he attacked the mother bear, and after some difficulty killed her. The cubs ran away. After the hunter dragged the bear home for his tribe, his friend continued to urge him to give up the bear hunt, but without success.

On another hunt, after a few days on the trail, the hunter met a stranger who informed him that near his village were a great many bears. "Every year many are killed by our hunters, but always there is an invincible one that has destroyed many of our hunters. Each time he kills a man, the bear tears him apart, examines him carefully as if searching for a special body mark. He is different because his feet and head are white."

They parted, and the hunter started out to look for that hunting ground. On his way, he stopped near a fish creek looking for game, but after a long night none appeared. Next morning he moved onward and came to a high bluff; below it he saw many bears on the tundra. He waited until some separated and looked over the remainder.

Among those, he saw the white-faced bear with white feet and concluded that this must be the ferocious, huge bear he sought. First he would keep an eye on it and wait for a favorable opportunity to kill it.

Now it seems that at one time, the white-faced bear was a human being and a very successful bear-hunter, too successful for his own good. His friends were envious and plotted to kill him. So they went to a medicine-man deep in the woods, and begged him to transform the successful hunter into a beast.

"Shoot a bear, skin it and place the skin under the pillow of your successful hunter," advised the Shaman.

After the bear-skin had been prepared, the Shaman and his friends quietly went to the man's hut and placed the skin under the man's pillow. They hid themselves to see what would happen when the man went to bed. Upon waking, the man found that he had become a huge bear with a white face and white feet.

"The white marks will show you which bear he is," said the Shaman, who disappeared into the woods.

Now our bear-hunter still sat at the edge of the bluff. Toward evening he saw the bears begin to leave, all except the white- faced bear. He was the last to get up, and he shook himself three times and acted as if he was deeply enraged. He moved toward the bluff where the hunter sat perfectly still. But the bear approached, and when he was almost face to face, asked, "What are you doing here?"

"I came out to hunt," he replied.

"Is it not enough that you have killed all my family, and recently killed my wife, and now you want to take my life? If you had injured my children the other day, I would now tear you to pieces. I will, however, spare your life this time on your promise that you will never hunt bears again. All the bears you saw today are my children and of my brother. Should I ever see you hunting bear, I will tear you apart."

Relieved to get away so easily, the hunter headed homeward. His friend met him and inquired about the white-faced bear, and when told what had happened, he urged the hunter to give up hunting. A whole week passed before the hunter set forth again, taking along six hunting friends.

For two days they hunted without luck, then came to the fish creek where they camped overnight. Next morning their leader took the six to the edge of the bluff where they could look down at the tundra and see many bears. But they could not see the white-faced bear and, encouraged, followed their leader toward the animals.

"Look at that strange-looking beast with white paws and a white face!" exclaimed one man.

The hunter-leader caught sight of that special bear and ordered his followers to retreat at once. So they went around another mountain where they saw many bears. They killed seven, one for each man.

Loaded with their spoil they took the homeward trail, but a short distance behind them they heard a commotion. They saw the white faced bear rapidly approaching them. The hunter aimed, but his bowstring broke. The others shot and missed. The white-faced bear spoke up and said, "Why do you shoot at me? I never harm you. Your leader killed my wife and nearly all my family. I warned him that if I found him hunting again, I would tear him apart. And this I shall do now, piece by piece. The rest of you can go. I'll not harm you because you have not harmed me."

Hurriedly, as fast as possible, the six men fled. The white-faced bear turned to the bear-hunter.

"I had you in my power once and I let you go on your promise not to hunt bear again. Now you are back at it and brought more bear-hunters along. This time I will do to you as you have done to mine."

The hunter pleaded to be allowed to live one more night so he could go home. At first the bear refused outright. The white-faced bear then relented, and would even spare his life entirely, if the hunter would tell him who had transformed him from a man into a beast. The hunter agreed to meet him the next night and go to the home of the Shaman.

When the bear-hunter reached home and found his six companions talking excitedly about the day's experience, they were surprised to see the hunter-leader alive.

The hunter told them his plan to meet the white-faced bear at the home of the Shaman next evening and asked the six to go with him. They refused and tried to dissuade their leader. But the bear- hunter kept his word and met the white-faced bear at the appointed place. A light shone from every hut except that of the Shaman.

"This is the place," said the man.

"I will remain here," ordered the bear. "You go inside and tell him there is a man outside wishing to speak with him."

The man advanced and found the skin-door tied, so he reported to the bear that the Shaman must be out. The bear ordered him back to cut the door, then walk in. Upon entering, the man heard someone call, "Who dares come into my lodge?"

"It is I," said the bear-hunter.

"What do you wish?"

"There is a man outside who wishes to speak to you."

Had the Shaman not been so sleepy, he might have been suspicious. Under the circumstances, his mind was not clear and he fell into the trap.

When the Shaman came near the white-faced bear, the old man became frightened and was ready to run away. But the bear blocked his way and said, "For years you have tortured me and made my life a burden in this condition. I demand you give me back my human form immediately, otherwise I shall tear you to pieces."

The Shaman promised to do so if the bear would follow him into his hut. Before going in, the bear said to the hunter, "Meet me here when I come out."

All night the Shaman worked hard with the bear, and by next morning succeeded in pulling off the bear-skin, and a human form appeared. The Shaman asked to keep the white-faced bear's skin, but the man kept the white-face and the white claws, which he cut off at once, giving the rest of the skin to the Shaman.

"If you ever again try to transform a man into a beast, I will be back and kill you dead, dead, dead," said the man.

The next day when the bear-man met the bear-hunter he said, "I caution you against ever going out to hunt bear. You may even hear people say I've become a bear again, and they will hunt me. Don't you join them. If I find you in their company, I will kill you dead, dead, dead."

For about four weeks the hunter remained at home with every intention of keeping his promise to the transformed man. But one day two young men from the neighboring tribal village came to beg his assistance. They asked his help to kill a ferocious bear with a white face and four white feet.

Of course the hunter knew the bear they feared, but decided to disguise himself and go help them. They gathered all of the village warriors and set out to find the white-faced bear. The bear saw them coming. He rose and shook himself three times, giving the impression of great anger, which frightened the warriors. Their chief said, "We are in great danger, so we must stand and fight."

Madly, the white-faced bear jumped, landed in front of the hunter and tore him to pieces. Then it pawed a hole in the ground and covered up the parts. The terrified warriors tried to escape, but the white-faced bear chased them back to their village, tearing them apart, killing all of them, including the old Shaman. Finished, the white-faced bear turned back into the woods to rest undisturbed forever.

How the Bear Lost His Tail

Adapted from Erminnie A. Smith, 1883, Myths of the Iroquois, Second Annual Report of the Bureau of American Ethnology

One winter, a fox saw a man dragging a sled full of fish that he had caught. The fox wanted some fish, so he tried to think of a way to get some of those fish on the sled. He went out to the path and lay down and pretended to be dead. The man came by and thought that the dead fox had nice fur, so he picked up the fox and put him on the sled with the fish. When the fisherman wasn't looking, the fox picked out several big fish and threw them off the sled and then jumped off himself. He had a good fish dinner and didn't have to get his feet wet.

The fox met a wolf and told him about tricking the fisherman, and the wolf decided to try it himself. The wolf lay down and pretended to be dead and let the fisherman find him, but the fisherman couldn't be tricked again. As the wolf was laying on the ground, the fisherman took a stick and whacked the wolf hard to make sure it was dead.

The wolf didn't like that and got up and ran away without getting any fish.

After his dinner, the fox also met a bear who wanted some fish. Together they went to the lake, which was frozen, and cut a hole in the ice to catch some fish. The fox told the bear, "Just put your tail down into the water and when the fish nibble on it, we'll get them." The bear sat and sat with his tail in the water but no fish nibbled at it. But it was so cold that the hole they had cut in the ice froze over and the bear's tail got stuck. He had to yank it out of the ice and he lost most of it in the ice, and so that is why the bear has a stumpy tail.

The Bear and the Rabbit Hunt Buffalo

Once upon a time there lived as neighbors, a bear and a rabbit. The rabbit was a good shot, and the bear being very clumsy could not use the arrow to good advantage. The bear was very unkind to the rabbit. Every morning, the bear would call over to the rabbit and say: "Take your bow and arrows and come with me to the other side of the hill. A large herd of buffalo are grazing there, and I want you to shoot some of them for me, as my children are crying for meat."

The rabbit, fearing to arouse the bear's anger by refusing, consented, and went with the bear, and shot enough buffalo to satisfy the hungry family. Indeed, he shot and killed so many that there was lots of meat left after the bear and his family had loaded themselves, and packed all they could carry home. The bear being very gluttonous, and not wanting the rabbit to get any of the meat, said: "Rabbit, you come along home with us and we will return and get the remainder of the meat."

The poor rabbit could not even taste the blood from the butchering, as the bear would throw earth on the blood and dry it up. Poor Rabbit would have to go home hungry after his hard day's work.

The bear was the father of five children. The youngest boy was very kind to the rabbit. The mother bear, knowing that her youngest was a very hearty eater, always gave him an extra large piece of meat. What the baby bear did not eat, he would take outside with him and pretend to play ball with it, kicking it toward the rabbit's house, and when he got close to the door, he would give the meat such a great kick, that it would fly into the rabbit's house, and in this way poor Rabbit would get his meal unknown to the papa bear.

Baby bear never forgot his friend Rabbit. Papa bear often wondered why his baby would go outside after each meal. He grew suspicious and asked the baby where he had been. "Oh, I always play ball outside, around the house, and when I get tired playing, I eat up my meat ball and then come in."

The baby bear was too cunning to let papa bear know that he was keeping his friend rabbit from starving to death. Nevertheless, papa bear suspected baby and said: "Baby, I think you go over to the rabbit's after every meal."

The four older brothers were very handsome, but baby bear was a little puny fellow, whose coat couldn't keep out much cold, as it was short and shaggy, and of a dirty brown color. The three older brothers were very unkind to baby bear, but the fourth one always took baby's part, and was always kind to his baby brother.

Rabbit was getting tired of being ordered and bullied around by papa bear. He puzzled his brain to scheme some way of getting even with Mr. Bear for abusing him so much. He studied all night long, but no scheme worth trying presented itself. Early one morning Mr. Bear presented himself at Rabbit's door.

"Say, Rabbit, my meat is all used up, and there is a fine herd of buffalo grazing on the hillside. Get your bow and arrows and come with me. I want you to shoot some of them for me."

"Very well," said Rabbit, and he went and killed six buffalo for Bear. Bear got busy butchering and poor Rabbit, thinking he would get a chance to lick up one mouthful of blood, stayed very close to the bear while he was cutting up the meat. The bear was very watchful lest the rabbit get something to eat. Despite bear's watchfulness, a small clot of blood rolled past and behind the bear's feet. At once Rabbit seized the clot and hid it in his bosom. By the time Rabbit got home, the blood clot was hardened from the warmth of his body, so, being hungry, it put Mr. Rabbit out of sorts to think that after all his trouble he could not eat the blood.

Very badly disappointed, he lay down on his floor and gazed up into the chimney hole. Disgusted with the way things had turned out, he grabbed up the blood clot and threw it up through the hole. Scarcely had it hit the ground when he heard the voice of a baby crying, "Ate! Ate!" (father, father). He went outside and there he found a big baby boy. He took the baby into his house and threw him out through the hole again. This time the boy was large enough to say "Ate, Ate, he-cun-sin-lo." (Father, father, don't do that). But nevertheless, he threw him up and out again. On going out the third time, there stood a handsome youth smiling at him. Rabbit at once adopted the youth and took him into his house, seating him in the seat of honor (which is directly opposite the entrance), and saying: "My son, I want you to be a good, honest, straightforward man. Now, I have in my possession a fine outfit, and you, my son, shall wear it."

Suiting his action to his words, he drew out a bag from a hollow tree and on opening it, drew out a fine buckskin shirt (tanned white as snow), worked with porcupine quills. Also, a pair of red leggings worked with beads. Moccasins worked with colored hair. A fine otter skin robe. White weasel skins to intertwine with his beautiful long black locks. A magnificent center eagle feather. A rawhide covered bow, accompanied by a quiver full of flint arrowheads.

The rabbit, having dressed his son in all the latest finery, sat back and gazed long and lovingly at his handsome son. Instinctively Rabbit felt that his son had been sent him for the purpose of being instrumental in the downfall of Mr. Bear. Events will show.

The morning following the arrival of Rabbit's son, Mr. Bear again presents himself at the door, crying out: "You lazy, ugly rabbit, get up and come out here. I want you to shoot some more buffalo for me."

"Who is this, who speaks so insultingly to you, father?" asked the son.

"It is a bear who lives near here, and makes me kill buffalo for his family, and he won't let me take even one little drop of blood from the killing, and consequently, my son, I have nothing in my house for you to eat."

The young man was anxious to meet Mr. Bear but Rabbit advised him to wait a little until he and Bear had gone to the hunt. So the son obeyed, and when he thought it time that the killing was done, he started out and arrived on the scene just as Mr. Bear was about to proceed with his butchering.

Seeing a strange shadow on the ground beside him, Mr. Bear looked up and gazed into the fearless eyes of rabbit's handsome son.

"Who is this?" asked Mr. Bear of poor little Rabbit.

"I don't know," answered Rabbit.

"Who are you?" asked the bear of Rabbit's son. "Where did you come from?"

The rabbit's son not replying, the bear spoke thus to him: "Get out of here, and get out quick, too."

At this speech the rabbit's son became angered, and fastened an arrow to his bow and drove the arrow through the bear's heart. Then he turned on Mrs. Bear and served her likewise. During the melee, Rabbit shouted: "My son, my son, don't kill the two youngest. The baby has kept me from starving and the other one is good and kind to his baby brother."

So the three older brothers who were unkind to their baby brother met a similar fate to that of their selfish parents.

This (the story goes) is the reason that bears travel only in pairs.

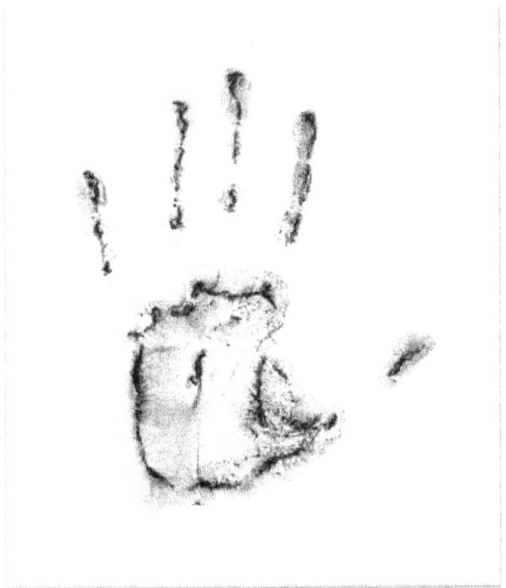

The Legend of the Bear Family

Penobscot

The story concerning the Bear family was revealed through a descendant of the original hero of the following tale. He owned a very old powder horn bearing an incised representation of his mother, who was a Bear, seated in the bow of a canoe travelling to the hunting grounds with her husband.

Many, many generations ago, a Penobscot, his wife, and their little son started out from their village to go to Canada. They were from Penobscot Bay, bound for a great council and dance to be held at the Iroquois village of Caughnawaga. They went upriver to the point where they had to make a 20-mile portage to reach another river that would take them to the St. Lawrence.

The man started ahead with the canoe on his back, leaving his wife to pack part of the luggage to their first overnight campsite. The little boy ran alongside of her. While she was busy arranging her pack, her son ran on ahead to catch up with his father.

The man had gone so far ahead, the boy became lost. The mother assumed the boy was with his father. When she arrived at the campground, they discovered that their son was with neither of them. They began a search immediately, but they could not find him.

The parents returned home to tell their story to their tribe. All of the men turned out for a wide search party, which lasted for several months without success. In March of the next year, the Penobscots found some sharpened sticks near the river. They concluded that the boy must be alive and had been spearing fish. Footprints of bears were seen, and they thought perhaps the boy had been adopted by a bear family.

In the village, there was a lazy man who did not enter into the search, but lay around idly. Everyone asked him, "Why don't you help hunt for the boy? You seem to be good for nothing."

"Very well, I will," he replied. He went right to the bear's den and knocked with his bow on the rocks at the entrance. Inside, a great noise arose where the father, mother, baby bear, and adopted boy lived. The father-bear went to the entrance, holding out a birch-bark vessel. The lazy man shot at it and killed the bear.

The mother-bear says, "Now I will go." She took another vessel, held it out at the entrance, and also was killed. The baby bear did the same and was killed. All of the bears were laid out dead in the cave. Then the lazy man entered and saw the little boy terribly afraid and huddled in a dark corner, crying for his relatives and trying to hide.

The lazy hunter gently carried him home to the village and gave him to his parents. Everyone gave the lazy man presents: two blankets, a canoe, ammunition, and other good things. He became rich overnight.

The boy's parents, however, noticed that their son seemed to be turning into a bear. Bristles were showing on his upper back and shoulders, and his manners had changed. Finally, they helped him to become a real person again, and he grew up to be a Penobscot Indian like his father. He married and had children. Forever after he and all of his descendants were called Bears.

They drew pictures of bears on pieces of birch-bark with charcoal and left them at camps wherever they went. All of their descendants seemed to do this and declare, "I am one of the Bear family."

Mooin, the Bear's Child

Now in the Old Time there lived a boy called Sigo, whose father had died when he was a baby. Sigo was too young to hunt and provide food for the wigwam, so his mother was obliged to take another husband, a jealous spiteful man who soon came to dislike his small stepson, for he thought the mother cared more for the child than for himself. He thought of a plan to be rid of the boy.

"Wife," said he, "it is time the boy learned something of the forest. I will take him with me today, hunting."

"Oh no!" cried his wife. "Sigo is far too young!"

But the husband snatched the boy and took him into the forest, while the mother wept, for she knew her husband's jealous heart.

The stepfather knew of a cave deep in the forest, a deep cave that led into a rocky hill. To this cave, he led his stepson and told him to go inside and hunt for the tracks of rabbit. The boy hung back.

"It is dark in there. I am afraid."

"Afraid!" scoffed the man. "A fine hunter you'll make," and he pushed the boy roughly into the cave. "Stay in there until I tell you to come out."

Then the stepfather took a pole and thrust it under a huge boulder so that it tumbled over and covered the mouth of the cave completely. He knew well there was no other opening. The boy was shut in for good and would soon die of starvation.

The stepfather left the place, intending to tell the boy's mother that her son had been disobedient, had run off and got lost, and he had been unable to find him. He would not return home at once. He would let time pass, as if he had been looking for the boy. Another idea occurred to him. He would spend the time on Blomidon's beach and collect some of Glooscap's purple stones to take as a peace offering to his wife. She might suspect, but nothing could be proved, and nobody would ever know what had happened.

Nobody? There was one who knew already. Glooscap the Great Chief was well aware of what had happened and he was angry, very angry. He struck his great spear into the red stone of Blomidon and the clip split. Earth and stones tumbled down, down, down to the beach, burying the wicked stepfather and killing him instantly.

Then Glooscap called upon a faithful servant, Porcupine, and told him what he was to do.

In the dark cave in the hillside, Sigo cried out his loneliness and fear. He was only six after all, and he wanted his mother. Suddenly he heard a voice.

"Sigo! Come this way."

He saw two glowing eyes and went towards them, trembling. The eyes grew bigger and brighter and at last he could see they belonged to an old porcupine.

"Don't cry any more, my son," said Porcupine. "I am here to help you," and the boy was afraid no longer. He watched as Porcupine went to the cave entrance and tried to push away the stone, but the stone was too heavy. Porcupine put his lips to the crack of light between boulder and hill side and called out:

"Friends of Glooscap! Come around, all of you!"

The animals and birds heard him and came--Wolf, Raccoon, Caribou, Turtle, Possum, Rabbit, and Squirrel, and birds of all kinds from Turkey to Hummingbird.

"A boy has been left here to die," called the old Porcupine from inside the cave. "I am not strong enough to move the rock. Help us or we are lost."

The animals called back that they would try. First Raccoon marched up and tried to wrap his arms around the stone, but they were much too short. Then Fox came and bit and scratched at the boulder, but he only made his lips bleed. Then Caribou stepped up and, thrusting her long antlers into the crack, she tried to pry the stone loose, but only broke off one of her antlers. It was no use. In the end, all gave up. They could not move the stone.

"Kwah-ee," a new voice spoke. "What is going on?" They turned and saw Mooinskw, which means she-bear, who had come quietly out of the woods. Some of the smaller animals were frightened and hid, but the others told Mooinskw what had happened. She promptly embraced the boulder in the cave's mouth and heaved with all her great strength. With a rumble and a crash, the stone rolled over. Then out came Sigo and Porcupine, joyfully.

Porcupine thanked the animals for their help and said, "Now I must find someone to take care of this boy and bring him up. My food is not the best for him. Perhaps there is someone here whose diet will suit him better. The boy is hungry--who will bring him food ?"

All scattered at once in search of food. Robin was the first to return, and he laid down worms before the boy, but Sigo could not eat them. Beaver came next, with bark, but the boy shook his head. Others brought seeds and insects, but Sigo, hungry as he was, could not touch any of them, At last came Mooinskw and held out a flat cake made of bluc berries. The boy seized it eagerly and ate.

"Oh, how good it is," he cried. And Porcupine nodded wisely.

"From now on," he said, "Mooinskw will be this boy's foster mother."

So Sigo went to live with the bears. Besides the mother bear, there were two boy cubs and a girl cub. All were pleased to have a new brother and they soon taught Sigo all their tricks and all the secrets of the forest, and Sigo was happy with his new-found family. Gradually, he forgot his old life. Even the face of his mother grew dim in memory and, walking often on all fours as the bears did, he almost began to think he was a bear.

One spring when Sigo was ten, the bears went fishing for smelts. Mooinskw walked into the water, seated herself on her haunches and commenced seizing the smelts and tossing them out on the bank to the children. All were enjoying themselves greatly when suddenly Mooinskw plunged to the shore, crying, "Come children, hurry!" She had caught the scent of man. "Run for your lives!"

As they ran, she stayed behind them, guarding them, until at last they were safe at home.

"What animal was that, Mother?" asked Sigo.

"That was a hunter," said his foster-mother, "a human like yourself, who kills bears for food." And she warned them all to be very watchful from now on. "You must always run from the sight or scent of a hunter."

Not long afterwards, the bear family went with other bear families to pick blueberries for the winter. The small ones soon tired of picking and the oldest cub had a sudden mischievous thought.

"Chase me towards the crowd," he told Sigo, "just as men do when they hunt bears. The others will be frightened and run away. Then we can have all the berries for ourselves."

So Sigo began to chase his brothers towards the other bears, whooping loudly, and the bears at once scattered in all directions. All, that is, except the mother bear who recognized the voice of her adopted son.

"Offspring of Lox!" she cried. "What mischief are you up to now?" And she rounded up the children and spanked them soundly, Sigo too.

So, the sun crossed the sky each day and the days grew shorter. At last, the mother bear led her family to their winter quarters in a large hollow tree. For half the winter they were happy and safe, with plenty of blueberry cakes to keep them from being hungry. Then, one sad day, the hunters found the tree.

Seeing the scratches on its trunk, they guessed that bears were inside, and they prepared to smoke them out into the open.

Mooinskw knew well enough what was about to happen and that not all would escape.

"I must go out first," she said, "and attract the man's attention, while you two cubs jump out and run away. Then you, Sigo, show yourself and plead for your little sister. Perhaps they will spare her for your sake."

And thus it happened, just as the brave and loving mother bear had said. As soon as she climbed down from the tree, the Indians shot her dead, but the two male cubs had time to escape. Then Sigo rushed out, crying:

"I am a human, like you. Spare the she-cub, my adopted sister."

The amazed Indians put down their arrows and spears and, when they had heard Sigo's story, they gladly spared the little she-bear and were sorry they had killed Mooinskw who had been so good to an Indian child.

Sigo wept over the body of his foster mother and made a solemn vow.

"I shall be called Mooin, the bear's son, from this day forwards. And when I am grown, and a hunter, never will I kill a mother bear, or bear children!"

And Mooin never did.

With his foster sister, he returned to his old village, to the great joy of his Indian mother, who cared tenderly for the she-cub until she was old enough to care for herself.

And ever since then, when Indians see smoke rising from a hollow tree, they know a mother bear is in there cooking food for her children, and they leave that tree alone.

The Bear Man

A Cherokee Story

A man went hunting in the mountains and came across a black bear, which he wounded with an arrow. The bear turned and started to run the other way, and the hunter followed, shooting one arrow after another into it without bringing it down.

Now, this was a medicine bear, and could talk or read the thoughts of people without their saying a word. At last he stopped and pulled the arrows out of his side and gave them to the man, saying, "It is of no use for you to shoot at me, for you can not kill me. Come to my house and let us live together."

The hunter thought to himself, "He may kill me;" but the bear read his thoughts and said, "No, I won't hurt you."

The man thought again, "How can I get anything to eat?" but the bear knew his thoughts, and said, "There shall be plenty." So the hunter went with the bear.

They went on together until they came to a hole in the side of the mountain, and the bear said, "This is not where I live, but there is going to be a council here and we will see what they do." They went in, and the hole widened as they went, until they came to a large cave like a townhouse.

It was full of bears--old bears, young bears, and cubs, white bears, black bears, and brown bears--and a large white bear was the chief. They sat down in a corner, but soon the bears scented the hunter and began to ask, "What is it that smells bad?"

The chief said, "Don't talk so; it is only a stranger come to see us. Let him alone."

Food was getting scarce in the mountains, and the council was to decide what to do about it. They had sent out messengers all over, and while they were talking two bears came in and reported that they had found a country in the low grounds where there, were so many chestnuts and acorns that mast was knee deep.

Then they were all pleased, and got ready for a dance, and the dance leader was the one the Indians call Kalâs'-gûnähi'ta, "Long Hams," a great black bear that is always lean.

After the dance the bears noticed the hunter's bow and arrows, and one said, "This is what men use to kill us. Let us see if we can manage them, and maybe we can fight man with his own weapons." So they took the bow and arrows from the hunter to try them. They fitted the arrow and drew back the string, but when they let go it caught in their long claws and the arrows dropped to the ground. They saw that they could not use the bow and arrows and gave them back to the man. When the dance and the council were over, they began to go home, excepting the White Bear chief, who lived there, and at last the hunter and the bear went out together.

They went on until they came to another hole in the side of the mountain, when the bear said, "This is where I live," and they went in. By this time the hunter was very hungry and was wondering how he could get something to eat. The other knew his thoughts and sitting up on his hind legs he rubbed his stomach with his forepaws--so--and at once he had both paws full of chestnuts and gave them to the man.

He rubbed his stomach again--so--and had his paws full of huckleberries, and gave them to the man. He rubbed again--so--and gave the man both paws full of blackberries. He rubbed again--so--and had his paws full of acorns, but the man said that he could not eat them, and that he had enough already.

The hunter lived in the cave with the bear all winter, until long hair like that of a bear began to grow all over his body and he began to act like a bear; but he still walked like a man. One day in early spring the bear said to him, "Your people down in the settlement are getting ready for a grand hunt in these mountains, and they will come to this cave and kill me and take these clothes from me"--he meant his skin--" but they will not hurt you and will take you home with them." The bear knew what the people were doing down in the settlement just as he always knew what the man was thinking about.

Some days passed and the bear said again, "This is the day when the Topknots will come to kill me, but the Split-noses will come first and find us. When they have killed me they will drag me outside the cave and take off my clothes and cut me in pieces. You must cover the blood with leaves, and when they are taking you away look back after you have gone a piece and you will see something."

Soon they heard the hunters coming up the mountain, and

then the dogs found the cave and began to bark. The hunters came and looked inside and saw the bear and killed him with their arrows. Then they dragged him outside the cave and skinned the body and cut it in quarters to carry home. The dogs kept on barking until the hunters thought there must be another bear in the cave.

They looked in again and saw the man away at the farther end. At first they thought it was another bear on account of his long hair, but they soon saw it was the hunter who had been lost the year before, so they went in and brought him out. Then each hunter took a load of the bear meat and they started home again, bringing the man and the skin with them.

Before they left the man piled leaves over the spot where they had cut up the bear, and when they had gone a little way he looked behind and saw the bear rise up out of the leaves, shake himself, and go back into the woods.

When they came near the settlement the man told the hunters that he must be shut up where no one could see him, without anything to eat or drink for seven days and nights, until the bear nature had left him and he became like a man again.

So they shut him up alone in a house and tried to keep very still about it, but the news got out and his wife heard of it. She came for her husband, but the people would not let her near him; but she came every day and begged so hard that at last after four or five days they let her have him. She took him home with her, but in a short time he died, because he still had a bear's nature and could not live like a man.

If they had kept him shut up and fasting until the end of the seven days, he would have become a man again and would have lived.

Turtle's Race with Bear

A Seneca Legend
Esquire Johnson, Seneca Chief, 1876

It was an early winter, cold enough so that the ice had frozen on all the ponds and Bear, who had not yet learned in those days that it was wiser to sleep through the White Season, grumbled as he walked through the woods.

Perhaps he was remembering a trick another animal had played on him, perhaps he was just not in a good mood. It happened that he came to the edge of a great pond and saw Turtle there with his head sticking out of the ice.

"Hah," shouted Bear, not even giving his old friend a greeting. "What are you looking at, Slow One?"

Turtle looked at Bear. "Why do you call me slow?"

Bear snorted. "You are the slowest of the animals. If I were to race you, I would leave you far behind." Perhaps Bear never heard of Turtle's big race with Beaver and perhaps Bear did not remember that Turtle, like Coyote, is an animal whose greatest speed is in his wits. "My friend," Turtle said, "let us have a race to see who is the swiftest."

"All right," said Bear. "Where will we race?"

"We will race here at this pond and the race will be tomorrow morning when the sun is the width of one hand above the horizon. You will run along the banks of the pond and I will swim in the water."

"How can that be?" Bear said. "There is ice all over the pond."

"We will do it this way," said Turtle. "I will make holes in the ice along the side of the pond and swim under the water to each hole and stick my head out when I reach it."

"I agree," said Bear. "Tomorrow we will race."

When the next day came, many of the other animals had gathered to watch. They lined the banks of the great pond and watched Bear as he rolled in the snow and jumped up and down making himself ready.

Finally, just as the sun was a hand's width in the sky, Turtle's head popped out of the hole in the ice at the starting line. "Bear," he called, "I am ready."

Bear walked quickly to the starting place and as soon as the signal was given, he rushed forward, snow flying from his feet and his breath making great white clouds above his head. Turtle's head disappeared in the first hole and then in almost no time at all reappeared from the next hole, far ahead of Bear.

"Here I am Bear," Turtle called. "Catch up to me!" And then he was gone again. Bear was astonished and ran even faster. But before he could reach the next hole, he saw Turtle's green head pop out of it.

"Here I am, Bear," Turtle called again. "Catch up to me!" Now bear began to run in earnest. His sides were puffing in and out as he ran and his eyes were becoming bloodshot, but it was no use. Each time, long before he would reach each of the holes, the ugly green head of Turtle would be there ahead of him calling out to him to catch up!

When Bear finally reached the finish line, he was barely able to crawl. Turtle was waiting there for him, surrounded by all the other animals. Bear had lost the race. He dragged himself home in disgrace, so tired that he fell asleep as soon as he reached his home. He was so tired that he slept until the warm breath of the Spring came to the woods again.

It was not long after Bear and all to other animals had left the pond that Turtle tapped on the ice with one long claw. At his sign it a dozen ugly heads like his popped up from the holes all along the edge of the pond. It was Turtle's cousins and brothers, all of whom looked just like him!

"My relatives," Turtle said, "I wish to thank you. Today we have shown Bear that it does not pay to call other people names. We have taught him a good lesson."

Turtle smiled and a dozen other turtles, all just like him, smiled back. "And we have shown the other animals," Turtle said, "that Turtles are not the slowest of the animals."

The Mother Bear's Song

Cherokee

A hunter in the woods one day heard singing in a cave. He came near and peeped in, and it was a mother bear singing to her cubs and telling them what to do when the hunters came after them.

Said the mother bear to the cubs, "When you hear the hunters coming down the creek, then-

Tsâ'gï, tsâ'gï, hwï'lahï';
(Upstream, upstream, you
must go) Tsâ'gï, tsâ'gï,
hwï'lahï. (Upstream,
upstream, you must go)

But if you hear them coming up the creek, children, then--

Ge'i, ge'i, hwï'lahï';
(Downstream, downstream,
you must go) Ge'i, ge'i,

hwĭ'lahĭ'" (Downstream,
downstream, you must go)

Another hunter out in the woods one day thought he heard a woman singing to a baby. He followed the sound up to the head of the branch until he came to a cave under the bushes, and inside was a mother bear rocking her cub in her paws and singing to it this baby song, which the Ani'-Tsâ'gûhĭ used to know before they were turned into bears:

Ha'-mama', ha'-mama', ha'-mama', ha'-mama'; (Let me carry you on my back, repeated four times)

Udâ'hale'yĭ hi'lûñnû, hi'lûñnû; (On the sunny side go to sleep, go to sleep)

Udâ'hale'yĭ hi'lûñnû, hi'lûñnû. (On the sunny side go to sleep, go to sleep)

Chipmunk and Bear

Iroquois Legend

Long ago when animals could talk, a bear was walking along. Now it has always been said that bears think very highly of themselves. Since they are big and strong, they are certain that they are the most important of the animals.

As this bear went along turning over big logs with his paws to look for food to eat, he felt very sure of himself. "There is nothing I cannot do," said this bear.

"Is that so?" said a small voice. Bear looked down. There was a little chipmunk looking up at Bear from its hole in the ground.

"Yes," Bear said, "that is true indeed." He reached out one huge paw and rolled over a big log. "Look at how easily I can do this. I am the strongest of all the animals. I can do anything. All the other animals fear me."

"Can you stop the sun from rising in the morning?" said the Chipmunk.

Bear thought for a moment. "I have never tried that," he said. "Yes, I am sure I could stop the sun from rising."

"You are sure?" said Chipmunk.

"I am sure," said Bear. "Tomorrow morning the sun will not rise. I, Bear, have said so." Bear sat down facing the east to wait.

Behind him the sun set for the night and still he sat there. The chipmunk went into its hole and curled up in its snug little nest, chuckling about how foolish Bear was. All through the night Bear sat. Finally the first birds started their songs and the east glowed with the light which comes before the sun.

"The sun will not rise today," said Bear. He stared hard at the glowing light. "The sun will not rise today."

However, the sun rose, just as it always had. Bear was very upset, but Chipmunk was delighted. He laughed and laughed. "Sun is stronger than Bear," said the chipmunk, twittering with laughter. Chipmunk was so amused that he came out of his hole and began running around in circles, singing this song:

"The sun came up,
The sun came up.
Bear is angry,
But the sun came up."

While Bear sat there looking very unhappy, Chipmunk ran around and around, singing and laughing until he was so weak that he rolled over on his back. Then, quicker than the leap of a fish from a stream, Bear shot out one big paw and pinned him to the ground.

"Perhaps I cannot stop the sun from rising," said Bear, "but you will never see another sunrise."

'Oh, Bear," said the chipmunk. "oh, oh, oh, you are the strongest, you are the quickest, you are the best of all of the animals. I was only joking." But Bear did not move his paw.

"Oh, Bear," Chipmunk said, "you are right to kill me, I deserve to die. Just please let me say one last prayer to Creator before you eat me."

"Say your prayer quickly," said Bear. "Your time to walk the Sky Road has come!"

"Oh, Bear," said Chipmunk, "I would like to die. But you are pressing down on me so hard I cannot breathe. I can hardly squeak. I do not have enough breath to say a prayer. If you would just lift your paw a little, just a little bit, then I could breathe. And I could say my last prayer to the Maker of all, to the one who made great, wise, powerful Bear and the foolish, weak, little Chipmunk.

"Bear lifted up his paw. He lifted it just a little bit. That little bit, though, was enough. Chipmunk squirmed free and ran for his hole as quickly as the blinking of an eye. Bear swung his paw at the little chipmunk as it darted away. He was not quick enough to catch him, but the very tips of his long claws scraped along Chipmunk's back leaving three pale scars.

To this day, all chipmunks wear those scars as a reminder to them of what happens when one animal makes fun to another.

Bear Spirits

Winnebago (Hotcâk) Legend

After Earthmaker created this island on which we live, he created all living things, man being the very last of these. The first and foremost animal that Earthmaker created was a bear of pure white color, whom he placed in the north. This is White Bear.

The second bear that he created was Red Bear, whom he placed in the west. Earthmaker next created in the east a kind of grizzly bear Blue Bear, who was the color of the sky, either blue, or as some say, gray. The last bear created by Earthmaker was Black Bear, who was placed in the south. These four kinds of bears were created as Island Weights to help stop the incessant spinning of the primordial earth.

Spiritually, they were not only bears, but the four cardinal winds as well. White Bear was chief over polar bears, Red Bear held hegemony over the brown bears of earth, Blue Bear ruled over Grizzlies, and Black Bear was chief of the terrestrial black bears.

If the white man wants to live in peace with the Indian, he can live in peace. Treat all men alike. Give them all the same law. Give them all an even chance to live and grow. All men were made by the same Great Spirit Chief. They are all brothers. The Earth is the mother of all people, and all people should have equal rights upon it. Let me be a free man, free to travel, free to stop, free to work, free to trade where I choose my own teachers, free to follow the religion of my fathers, free to think and talk and act for myself, and I will obey every law, or submit to the penalty.
Native American Quote

Peace and happiness are available in every moment. Peace is every step. We shall walk hand in hand. There are no political solutions to spiritual problems. Remember: If the Creator put it there, it is in the right place. The soul would have no rainbow if the eyes had no tears.
Native American Quote

When we show our respect for other living things, they respond with respect for us.
Arapaho Proverb

Adventures of Coyote

A Cougar Tale

Dorsey, George A. Traditions of the Caddo. Washington: Carnegie Institution. 1905

In the beginning of the world there were many, many people, and the people held councils to decide how things should be. There was one man, named Coyote, who always had something to say on every subject. At one council this question came up: "How and what kind of rain should be in the world?" One of the men said that it should rain in the form of lead balls, which would be very dangerous, and so when the rain came the people would have to stay at home. Then Coyote arose from his seat and said: "If it should rain nothing but lead it would be very dangerous for my people, because they do not stay at home very much, and as for myself, I might be carrying a big deer to my family to eat when the rain begins to fall and I would certainly be killed. I say, let it rain in drops of water. Then we can be caught out in the rain and get very wet, but we will soon be dry again, and the wetting will be good for us." The people accepted Coyote's suggestion, and so it is that it rains in the form of water.

When the council was all over and the people went to their homes, Coyote made up his mind to go out and visit some of his friends. He traveled until he came to the mountains. He saw smoke coming up among the mountains, as though some one was making up a big fire, and he thought he would go up and see who was living there. When he came near to the place, he saw some one sitting by the fire. It was the great, powerful Bear. Coyote went closer, and Bear asked him if he was the person who was called Coyote, and Bear told him that if he was that he was going to kill him, for he had heard many bad things about him. Coyote told Bear he was not the person, but that he was the son of a great and powerful medicine-man. Bear did not believe him and decided to kill him.

When he was about to kill him, Coyote told him to wait until his father saw him, for he might have something to say to him before he died. This happened at sunrise, and when the sun was just peeping over the hilltops Coyote said to Bear: "Now you may kill me or do as you please with me, because my father is watching me." Then Bear began to back away, and as he did so, Coyote began to go nearer and nearer to Bear. Finally, he began to push him with his elbow, at the same time saying: "Now kill me while my father is watching me." Bear thought that he must be a great man, if he was the son of the Sun, and he wondered how he received his powers from the Sun. He became frightened and gave Coyote many things to eat, and then Coyote told Bear to come and make him a visit some time, whenever he felt like going anywhere. A long while after this, Bear found out that the person who made a visit to him was not the son of the Sun, but that he was the man Coyote, whom he wanted to kill. Bear was more angry at him than ever, and so he thought he would fool Coyote some way by going and visiting him and killing him if he could find his home. Bear did not find his home, because Coyote was always moving from place to place, for he knew that Bear was after him, and that he would kill him if he could catch him.

While Coyote was moving from one place to another he came down to a large lake of clear, cool water, and after he had been there for some time, he started off a little way from the lake. While gone he saw some one coming up toward him and, as he was very cowardly, he started to run away. The person was not his enemy, but a friend of his, Mountain-Lion. He called Coyote back, and so he came, and he told his friend that he was very hungry, for he had had nothing to eat for a long while. Mountain-Lion asked him to go along with him, saying that he would find something for him to eat soon.

They both went to the lake, and when they came down to the water Mountain-Lion told Coyote that he was going to kill a young horse. In those times there were many herds of wild horses, and at the lake there was a certain place where the wild horses drank. Near the place where the road led to the water there was a large tree, and the horses passed under the tree as they went down to the water. Every day at about noon Mountain-Lion would climb the tree and then pounce down on a young horse and kill him. As Mountain-Lion and Coyote drew near to the tree Mountain-Lion told Coyote to place himself where the wild herd of horses could not see him, and so he did, and Mountain-Lion climbed the tree. Soon Coyote saw dust rise up from the ground and he heard something like thundering, and later he saw many hundreds of horses coming down to the water.

As the horses were passing under the tree, Coyote saw Mountain-Lion jump out of the tree and pounce upon a young horse and kill it. Then Mountain-Lion and Coyote both had a fine dinner. That day, after they had eaten, Mountain-Lion told Coyote to continue on his way; but Coyote did not want to leave his friend, and so he asked Mountain-Lion if he could give him power so that he could kill a horse, too, and eat it when he was hungry. Mountain-Lion told him he would. They stayed there until the next day, and at about noon they both went down to the lake again, and went to the tree, and then Mountain-Lion showed Coyote how and what to do when the horses should come. He taught him how to climb the tree, and then he went out to place himself where the horses could not see him.

Soon they began to come from different directions, and as they filed down to the water Coyote picked out a fat young horse, and as they were coming up from the water, he jumped on it and killed it. They had another fine dinner, and then Mountain-Lion said to Coyote: "Do not try to kill a three or four-year-old horse. If you jump on one that is three years old you cannot kill him and you may lose your own life. Try to kill one that is one or two years old and you will succeed every time."

Coyote left his new friend and went on his way. The next day, while he was alone, he began to get very hungry, and so at about noon he went down to the lake to kill a horse. While he was on the tree, he said to himself: "I wonder if it would be dangerous for me to kill one of the large horses. I may be stronger than Mountain-Lion, and so I will try to kill the largest horse and I will show Mountain-Lion that I am not so small as I look to him."

The horses began to go down to the water, and Coyote waited and waited for the chance to jump upon the largest horse in the herd. Finally, a large horse came, and when he was right under the tree Coyote jumped upon him. It was but a short time until the horse threw Coyote off from his back, and when Coyote was down on the ground the horse kicked him under the jaws and went off.

As Coyote was about to die, Mountain-Lion, who had been watching Coyote all the time, came up to see what was the matter with him, and when he came up to him, he saw his jaws to one side. Mountain-Lion asked Coyote what he was laughing about, and asked him if he was able to kill another five-year-old horse. Coyote lay there for a long time before he was able to move.

Finally, he arose and decided to leave the place, never to return to it. As he was going along a small stream, he heard some one up in a persimmon tree, and so he thought that he would go over and see who it was. He found Opossum in the persimmon tree eating persimmons.

Coyote went under the tree and asked Opossum to throw down some persimmons to him. Opossum refused and laughed at Coyote and began to play with him. Opossum would take one persimmon and eat it, and then he would throw the seeds down to Coyote.

Finally, Coyote became angry at Opossum and wished he could get him down from the tree. Sometimes Opossum would get on a small limb of the tree, and then drop down as though he was going to fall to the ground, but he would always catch himself by wrapping his tail around the limb. He kept on doing this to torment Coyote for a long time, until he climbed out on a dry limb. He threw himself off the limb again and said to Coyote: “I am falling off, sure. I am coming down,” and just as he let himself off of the limb it broke off and down came Opossum.

Coyote was upon him and gave him a good beating, and then he left him to die. Opossum fooled Coyote, for he was not hurt at all, and when Coyote went away Opossum jumped up and climbed the persimmon tree again. After a while Coyote looked back to see if Opossum was dead. He could not see him, and so he went back and found that Opossum was gone. He looked up in the tree, and there he saw him laughing at him again.

Bear Did Not Always Hibernate

An American Indian Legend - Nation Unknown

The bear is a giant of a beast, but gentle to all who see its tender loving ways. The bear did not always sleep (hibernate).

It was during the time of the first winter that Wind gave Bear the gift of sleep. All the animals of the forest thought Bear was lazy and slow. They would tease him and harass the poor soul daily. They viewed his kind gentle ways as a weakness.

They always laughed at his friends, and when he stopped and talked to them. Still Bear did not hate or get angry at the animals who made fun of him, he just smiled and went on his way. He loved his feathered friends, his underground friends and his underwater friends. The only time he was sad is when he was hungry and had to eat one of them.

One day father Wind heard all the animals talking about how foolish bear was. Even Fish turned against his friend. This made Wind very mad.

In a dream he taught Bear what plants to eat and all about the bad things Fish had said. He told Bear fish was not a friend but food. He also told Bear that because he was kind he would receive a special gift. Then bear awoke wondering what gift would Wind give him.

In the next dream, Bear was sad. Winter asked him what is wrong? "I am only good because I have good friends". "That is true", said Winter. So, he told Bear to go and tell all his friends about the gift that Wind had promised him.

When Bear awoke, he ran through the forest and told all who would listen. This made him very tired and sleepy so he went back to cave and fell asleep.

As before, many creatures did not listen to Bear. They went about their business. Some even called him crazy. So, Winter decided to teach them a lesson. As Bear and his friends slept, flew away, or gathered food, without knowing Winter came down upon the forest. Yet, he made sure that those who were friends of Bear were not aware of him or his brother Wind. To them it was a time of the gift.

So as Winter begins his journey across the land, one can still see who were the friends of Bear...Are You???

The Rabbit Dines the Bear

Cherokee Legend

The Bear invited the Rabbit to dine with him. They had beans in the pot, but there was no grease for them, so the Bear cut a slit in his side and let the oil run out until they had enough to cook the dinner.

The Rabbit looked surprised, and thought to himself, "That's a handy way. I think I'll try that."

When he started home, he invited the Bear to come and take dinner with him four days later.

When the Bear came the Rabbit said, "I have beans for dinner, too. Now I'll get the grease for them." So he took a knife and drove it into his side, but instead of oil, a stream of blood gushed out and he fell over nearly dead.

The Bear picked him up and had hard work to tie up the wound and stop the bleeding. Then he scolded him, "You little fool, I'm large and strong and lined with fat all over; the knife don't hurt me; but you're small and lean, and you can't do such things."

How the Summer Birds Came

Zuni Legend
Frank Hamilton Cushing, Zuni Folk Tales, 1901

In the days of the ancients, in the town under Thunder Mountain called K'iákime, there lived a most beautiful maiden. But one thing which struck the people who knew her was that she seldom came forth from her room.

She never went out of her house; never seemed to care for the people around her, never seemed to care to see the young men when they were dancing.

Now, this was the way of it. Through the roof of her room was a little skylight, open, and when it rained, one of the Gods of the Rain descended in the rain-drops and wooed this maiden, and married her all unknown to her people; so that she was in his company every time it rained, and when the dew fell at night, on his ladder of water descending he came, and she was very happy, and cared not for the society of men. By-and-by, behold! to the utter surprise of the people, whose eyes could not see this god, her husband, there was a little boy born to her.

Now, he was the child of the gods, and, therefore, before he was many days old, he had begun to run about and speak, and had wonderful intelligence and wonderful strength and vivacity. He was only a month or two old when he was like a child of five or six or eight years of age, and he would climb to the house-top and run down into the plaza and out around the village hunting birds or other small animals.

With only his fingers and little stones for weapons, he never failed to slay and bring home these little creatures, and his mother's house was supplied more than any other house in the town with plumes for sacrifice, from the birds which he captured in this way.

Finally, he observed that the older men of the tribe carried bows and arrows, and that the arrows went more swiftly and straighter than the stones he threw; and though he never failed to kill small animals, he found he could not kill the larger ones in that way. So he said to his mother one night: "Oh, mother, where does the wood grow that they make bows of, and where do they get sticks for their arrows? I wish you would tell me."

But the mother was quite silent; she didn't like to tell him, for she thought it would lead him away from the town and something would happen to him. But he kept questioning her until at last, weary with his importunities, she said: "Well, my little boy, if you go round the cliff here to the eastern side, there is a great hollow in the rocks, and down at the bottom of that hollow is a great cave.

Now, around that shelter in the rocks are growing the trees

out of which bows are made, and there also grow the bushes from which arrows are cut; they are so plentiful that they could supply the whole town, and furnish all the hunters here with bows and arrows; but they cannot get them, because in the cave lives a great Bear, a very savage being, and no one dares go near there to get timber for the bows or sticks for the arrows, because the Bear would surely devour whoever ventured there. He has devoured many of our people; therefore, you must not go there to get these arrows.

"No, indeed," said the boy. But at night he lay down with much in his mind, and was so thoughtful that he hardly slept the whole night. He was planning what he would do in the morning.

The next morning his mother was busy about her work, and finally she went down to the spring for some water, and the little boy slipped out of the house, ran down the ladder, went to the riverside, stooped down, and crawled along the bank of the river, until he could get around on the side of the cliff where the little valley of the spring that flows under Thunder Mountain lies.

There he climbed up and up until he came to the shelter in the rocks round on the eastern side of Thunder Mountain. The mouth of this hollow was entirely closed with fine yellow-wood and oak, the best timber we have for bows, and straight sprouts were growing everywhere out of which arrows could be made.

"Ah, this must be the place," said the boy, as he looked at it. “I don't see any Bear. I think I will climb up and see if there is anything to be afraid of, and try if I can cut a stick before the Bear comes out."

He started and climbed into the mouth of the cavern, and his father, one of the Gods of the Rain, threw a tremendous shaft of lightning, and it thundered, and the cave closed together.

"Ha!" cried the boy. "What in the world is the meaning of this?" Then he stood there a moment, and presently the clouds finished and the cave opened, and all was quiet. He started to go in once more, and down came the lightning again, to remind him that he should not go in there.

"Ha!" cried the boy again. "What in the world does it mean?" And he rubbed his eyes, it had rather stunned him, --and so soon as it had cleared away he tried again, and again for the fourth time.

Finally, the god said, "Ah! I have reminded him and he does not heed. He must go his own way." So the boy climbed into the cave.

No sooner had he got in than it began to get dark, and Wah! came the Bear on his hind legs and grabbed the boy and began to squeeze him very tight.

"O my! O my!" cried he. Don't squeeze me so hard! It hurts; don't squeeze me so hard! My mother is one of the most beautiful women you ever saw!"

"Hollo!" exclaimed the Bear. "What is that you say?"

"My mother is one of the most beautiful women you ever saw!"

"Indeed!" said the Bear, as he relaxed his hold.

"My son, sit down. What did you come to my house for? I am sure you are very welcome."

"Why," said the boy, "I came to get a piece of wood for a bow and sticks for arrows."

Said the Bear, "I have looked out for this timber for a long time. There is none better in the whole country. Let me tell you what I will do. You don't look very strong. You haven't anything to cut the trees down with. I will go myself and cut down a tree for you. I will pick out a good one for a bow; not only that, but I will get fine sticks for arrows, too. So he stalked off into the forest, and crack, crack, he smashed the trees down, and, picking out a good one, gnawed off the ends of it and brought it to the boy, then gathered a lot of fine straight sticks for arrow-shafts and brought them.

"There," said he, "take those home. Do you know how to make a bow, my son?"

"No, I don't very well," replied he.

"Well," said the Bear, "I have cut off the ends; make it about that length. Now take it home, and shave down the inside until it is thin enough to bend quickly at both ends, and lay it over the coals of fire so it will get hard and dry. That is the way to make a good bow."

"All right," said the boy; and as he took up the bundle of sticks and the stave for the bow, he said: "just come along toward night and I will introduce you to my mother."

"All right," said the old Bear; "I will be along just about sunset. Then I can look at your bow and see whether you have made it well or not."

So the boy trudged home with his bundle of sticks and his bow stave, and when he arrived there his mother happened to be climbing out, and saw him coming.

"You wretched boy," she said, "I told you not to go out to the cave! I warrant you have been there where the Bear stays!"

"Oh, yes, my mother; just see what I have brought," said the boy. "I sold you to the Bear. He will be here to get you this evening. See what I have brought!" and he laid out his bow-timber and arrow-shafts.

"Oh," said she, "you are the most wretched and foolish of little boys; you pay no attention to what any one says to you; your mother's word is nothing but wind in your ears." "Just see what I have brought home," said he. He worked as hard as he could to make his bow, stripped the arrow-shafts, smoothed and straightened them before the fire, and made the points of obsidian… very black it is; very hard and sharp were the points when he placed them on the arrows. Now, after placing the feathers on the arrows, he stood them up on the roof of the house against the parapet in the sunlight to dry; and he had his bow on the other side of the house against the other parapet to dry. He was still at work, toward sunset, when he happened to look up and saw the Bear coming along, slowly, comfortably, rolling over the sand.

"Ah!" said he, "the old man is coming." He paid no attention to him, however.

Presently the Bear came close to the ladder, and shook it to see if it was strong enough to hold him. "Thou comest?" asked the boy. "Yes," said the Bear. "How have you been all day?" "Happy," said the boy. "How is your mother?" "Happy," said the boy, "expecting you." So the old Bear climbed up. "Ah, indeed," said he, as he got over the edge of the house, "have you made the bow?" "Yes, after a fashion." So the Bear went over, raised himself on his hind feet, looked at the bow, pulled it, and said, as he laid it down: "It is a splendid bow. What is this black stuff on these arrows?" "Obsidian," answered the boy. "These points are nothing but black coals," said the Bear. "I tell you," said the boy, "they are good, black, flint arrow-heads, hard and sharp as any others." "No," said the other, "nothing but coals." "Now, suppose you let me try one of those coals on you," said the boy. "All right," said the Bear. He walked over to the other side of the roof and stood there, and the boy took one of the arrows, fitted it to the bow, and let go. It went straight into the heart of the Bear, and even passed through him entirely. "Wah!" uttered the Bear, as he gave a great snort and rolled over on the house-top and died.

"Ha, ha!" shouted the boy, "what you had intended to do unto me, thus unto you! Oh, mother!" called he, as he ran to the skyhole, "here is your husband; come and see him. I have killed him; but, then, he would have me make the experiment," said the boy.

"Oh, you foolish, foolish, disobedient boy!" said the mother. What have you been doing now? Are we safe? "Oh, yes," said he; "my step-father is as passive as if he were asleep." And he went on and skinned his once prospective step-father, and then took out his heart and hung it to the cross-piece of the ladder as a sign that the people could go and get all the bow-timber and arrows they pleased.

That night, after the evening meal was over, the boy sat down with his mother, and he said: "By the way, mother, are there any monsters or fearful creatures anywhere round about this country that kill people and make trouble?"

"No," said the mother, "none whatever."

"I don't know about that; I think there must be," said the boy.

"No, there are none whatever, I tell you," answered the mother.

The boy began to tumble on the floor, rolling about, playing with his mother's blankets, and throwing things around, and once in a while he would ask her again the same question, until finally she got very cross with him and said: "Yes, if you want to know, down there in the valley, beyond the great plains of sagebrush, is a den of Misho Lizards who are fearful and deadly to every one who goes near them. Therefore, you had better be careful how you run round the valley."

"What makes them so fearful?" asked he.

"Well," said she, "they are venomous; they have a way of throwing from their mouths or breath a sort of fluid which, whenever it strikes a person, burns him, and whenever it strikes the eyes it blinds them.

A great many people have perished there. Whenever a man arrives at their den they are very polite and greet him most courteously; they say: 'Come in; sit down right here in the middle of the floor before the fire.' But as soon as the person is seated in their house they gather round the walls and throw this venom on him, and he dies almost immediately."

"Is it possible?" responded the little boy; and for some reason or other he began to grow sleepy, and said: "Now, let us go to sleep, mother." So he lay down and slept. Just as soon as it was light the next morning he aroused himself, dressed, took his bow and arrows, and, placing them in a corner near the ladder, said: "Oh, mother, give me my breakfast; I want to go and shoot some little birds. I would like to have some roasted birds for dinner."

She gave him his breakfast as quickly as she could, and he ran down the ladder and went to shooting at the birds, until he happened to see that his mother and others were out of sight; then he skulked into the sagebrush and went as straight as he could for the den of the Misho Lizards. There happened to be two young ones sunning themselves outside, and they said:

"Ah, my fine little fellow, glad to see you this morning. Come in, come in; the old ones will be very much pleased to entertain you. Come in!"

"Thank you," said the boy. He walked in, but he felt under his coat to see if a huge lump of rock salt he had was still there.

"Sit right down here," said the old people. The whole den was filled with these Misho Lizards, and they were excessively polite, every one of them.

The boy sat down, and the old Misho said to the young ones: "Hurry up, now; be quick!" And they began to throw their venom at him, and continued until he was all covered with it; but, knowing beforehand, and being the child of the gods, he was prepared and protected, and it did him no harm.

"Thank you, thank you," said the boy. "I will do the same thing.

Then he pulled out the salt and pushed it down into the fire, where it exploded and entirely used up the whole council of Misho Lizards.

"There!" cried the boy. "Thus would you have done unto me, thus unto you."

He took two fine ones and cut out their hearts, then started for home. When he arrived there, he climbed the ladder and suspended the two hearts beside that of the Bear and went down into the house, saying, "Well, mother, is dinner ready?"

"There now," said she, "I know it. I saw you hang those hearts up. You have been down there."

"Yes," said he, "they are all gone--every solitary one of them."

"Oh, you foolish, foolish, disobedient fellow! I am all alone in the world, and if you should go to some of those fearful places some time and not comeback, who would hunt for me? What should I do?" said the mother.

"Don't be troubled, mother, now," said the boy. "I don't think I will go any more. There is nothing else of that kind around, is there, mother?"

"No, there is not," she replied; "not a thing. There may be somewhere in the world, but there is not anywhere here."

In the evening, as he sat with his mother, the boy kept questioning and teasing her to tell him of some other monsters--pulling on her skirts and repeating his questions.

"I tell you," she said, "there are no such creatures."

"Oh, mother, I know there are," said he, "and you must tell me about them."

So he continued to bother her until her patience gave out,

and she told him of another monster.

Said she: "If you follow that cañon down to the southeast, there is a very, very, very high cliff there, and the trail that goes over that cliff runs close by the side of a precipice. Now, that has been for ages a terrible place, for there is a Giant living there, who wears a hairknot on his forehead. He lies there at length, sunning himself at his ease.

He is very good-natured and very polite. His legs stretch across the trail on which men have to go who pass that way, and there is no other way to get by. And whenever a man tries to go by that trail, he says: 'Pass right along, pass right along; I am glad to see you. Here is a fresh trail; some one has just passed. Don't disturb me; I am sunning myself.' Down below is the den where his children live, and on the flesh of these people he feeds them."

"Mercy!" exclaimed the boy. "Fearful! I never shall go there, surely. That is too terrible! Come, let us go to sleep; I don't want to hear anything more about it."

But the next morning, just as soon as daylight appeared, he got up, dressed himself, and snatched a morsel of food.

His mother said to him: "Where are you going? Are you thinking of that place I told you about?"

"No," said he; "I am going to kill some prairie-dogs right here in sight. I will take my war-club."

So he took his war-club, and thrust it into his belt in front, ran down the hill on which the village stood, and straightway went off to the place his mother had told him of.

When he reached the top of the rocks he looked down, and

there, sure enough, lay the Giant with the forehead knot.

The Giant looked up and said: "Ah, my son, glad to see you this morning; glad to see you coming so early. Some one just passed here a little while ago; you can see his tracks there."

"Well," said the boy, "make room for me."

"Oh, just step right over," said the old man; "step right over me."

"I can't step over your great legs," said the boy; "draw them up."

"All right," said the old Demon. So, he drew his knees up. "There, now, there is plenty of room; pass right along, my son."

Just as the boy got near the place, he thrust out his leg suddenly that way, to kick him off the cliff; but the boy was too nimble for him, and jumped aside.

"Oh, dear me," cried the Monster; "I had a stitch in my leg; I had to stretch it out."

"Ah," said the boy, "you tried to kick me off, did you?"

"Oh, no," said the old villain I had a terrible stitch in my knee,"--and he began to knead his knee in the most vehement manner. "just pass right along; I trust it won't happen again." The boy again attempted to pass, and the same thing happened as before.

"Oh, my knee! my knee!" exclaimed the Monster.

"Yes, your knee, your knee!" said the boy, as he whipped

out his war-club and whacked the Giant on the head before he had time to recover himself. "Thus unto me you would have done, thus unto you!" said the boy.

No sooner had the Giant fallen than the little Top-knots gathered round him and began to eat; and they ate and ate and ate, --there were many of them, and they were voracious--until they came to the top-knot on the old fellow's head, and then one of them cried; "Oh, dear, alas and alas! this is our own father!"

And while they were still crying, the boy cut out the Giant's heart and slung it over his shoulder; then he climbed down the cliff to where the young Top-knots were, and slew them all except two, --a pair of them. Then he took these two, who were still young, like little children, and grasping one by the throat, wrung its neck and threw it into the air, when it suddenly became a winged creature, and spread out its wings and soared away, crying: "Peep, peep, peep," just as the falcons of today do. Then he took the other one by the neck, and swung it round and round, and flung it into the air, and it flew away with a heavy motion, and cried: "Boohoo, boohoo, boohoo!" and became an owl.

"Ah," said the boy, "born for evil, changed for good! Ye shall be the means whereby our children in the future shall sacrifice to the gods themselves."

Then he trudged along home with the Giant's heart, and when he got there, he hung it on the cross-piece of the ladder by the side of the other hearts. It was almost night then.

"There, now!" said his mother, as he entered the house; "I have been troubled almost to death by your not coming home sooner. You went off to the place I told you of; I know you did!"

"Ha!" said he, "of course I did. I went up there, and the poor fellows are all dead."

"Why will you not listen to me?" said she.

"Oh, it is all right, mother," said the boy. "It is all right." She went on scolding him in the usual fashion, but he paid no attention to her.

As soon as she had sat down to her evening tasks, he asked: "Now, is there any other of these terrible creatures?"

"Well, I shall tell you of nothing more now," said she.

"Why, is there anything more?" asked the boy.

"No, there is not," replied she.

"Ah, mother, I think there must be."

"No; there is nothing more, I tell you." "Ah, mother, I think there must be." And he kept bothering and teasing until she told him again (she knew she would have to): "Yes, away down in the valley, some distance from here, near the little Cold-making Hill, there lives a fearful creature, a four-fold Elk or Bison, more enormous than any other living thing.

Awiteli Wakashi he is called, and no one can go near him. He rushes stamping and bellowing about the country, and people never pass through that section from fear." "Ah," said the boy don't tell me any more he must be a fearful creature, indeed." "Yes; but you will be sure to go there," said she.

"Oh, no, no, mother; no, indeed!" But the next morning he

went earlier than ever, carrying with him his bows and arrows. He was so filled with dread, however, or pretended to be, that as he went along the trail he began to cry and sniffle, and walk very slowly, until he came near the hole of an old Gopher, his grandfather.

The old fellow was working away, digging another cellar, throwing the dirt out, when he heard this crying. Said he: "That is my grandson; I wonder what he is up to now." So he ran and stuck his nose out of the hole he was digging, and said: "Oh, my grandchild, where are you doing?" The boy stopped and began to look around. "Right here! right here!" cried the grandfather, calling his attention to the hole. "Come, my boy." The boy put his foot in, and the hole enlarged, and he went down into it. "Now, dry your eyes, my grandchild, and tell me what is the matter." "Well," said the boy, "I was going to find the four-fold Bison. I wanted to take a look at him, but I am frightened!" "Why, what is the matter? Why do you not go?" said the Gopher. "Well, to tell you the truth, I thought I would try to kill him," he answered. "Well, I will do what I can to help; you had better not try to do it alone. Sit here comfortably; dry your eyes, and I will see what I can do." The old Gopher began to dig, dig, dig under the ground for a long way, making a fine tunnel, and packed it hard on the top and sides so that it would not fall in.

He finally came to hear the "thud, thud, thud" of the heart of this creature, where it was lying, and dug the hole up to that spot. When he got there he saw the long layers of hair on its body, where no arrow could penetrate, and he cut the hair off, so that the skin showed white.

Then he silently stole back to where the boy was and said: "Now, my boy, take your bow and arrows and go along through this hole until you get to where the tunnel turns upward, and then, if you look well, you will see a light patch. That is the skin next the heart of the four-fold Bison. He is sleeping there. You will hear the 'thud, thud, thud' of his heart. Shoot him exactly in the middle of that place, and then, mind you, turn around and run for your life, and the moment you get to my hole, tumble in, headforemost or any way."

So the boy did as he was told-crawled through the tunnel until he came to where it went upward, saw the light patch, and let fly an arrow with all his might, then rushed and scrambled back as hard as he could.

With a roar that shook the earth the four-fold Bison fell over, then struggled to his feet, snorted, bellowed, and stuck his great horn into the tunnel, and like a flash of fire ripped it from end to end, just as the boy came tumbling into the deeper hole of his grandfather.

"Ah!" exclaimed the Gopher.

"He almost got me," said the boy.

"Sit still a moment and rest, my grandson," said the Gopher. "He didn't catch you. I will go and see whether he is dead."

So the Gopher stuck his nose out of the hole and saw there a great heap of flesh lying. He went out, nosed around, and smelt, jumped back, and went forward again until he came to the end of the creature, and then he took one of his nails and scratched out an eye, and there was no sign of life. So he ran back to the boy, and said: "Yes, he breathes no more; you need not fear him longer."

"Oh, thank you, my grandfather!" said the boy.

And he climbed out, and laid himself to work to skin the beast. He took off its great thick skin, and cut off a suitable piece of it, for the whole pelt was so large and heavy that he could not carry it; then he took out the animal's great heart, and finally one of the large intestines and filled it with blood, then started for home.

He went slowly, because his load was so heavy, and when he arrived he hung the heart on the ladder by the side of the others, and dragged the pelt to the skyhole, and nearly scared the wits out of his mother by dropping it into the room.

"Oh, my child, now, here you are! Where have you been?" cried she. "I warned you of the place where the four-fold Bison was; I wonder that you ever came home." "Ah, the poor creature said the boy he is dead. just look at this. He isn't handsome any more; he isn't strong and large any more."

"Oh, you wretched, wretched boy! You will be the death of me, as well as of yourself, some time," said the mother.

"No, mother," said the boy; "that is all nonsense."

That evening the boy said to his mother: "Now, mother, is there anything else of this kind left? If there is, I want to know it. Now, don't disappoint me by refusing to tell."

Oh, my dear son," said she, "I wish you wouldn't ask me; but indeed there is. There are terrible birds, great Eagles, fearful Eagles, living over on Shuntekia. In the very middle of an enormous cliff is a hollow place in the rocks where is built their nest, and there are their young ones. Day after day, far and near, they catch up children and young men and women, and carry them away, never more to be seen.

These birds are more terrible than all the rest, because how can one get near to slay them? My son, I do hope and trust that you will not go this time, --but, you foolish little boy, I see that you will go."

"Well, mother, let us go to sleep, and never mind anything about it," said the boy.

But after his mother had gone to sleep, he took the piece of rawhide he had skinned from the fourfold Bison, and, cutting it out, made himself a suit--a green rawhide suit, skin-tight almost, so that it was perfectly smooth. Then he scraped the hair off, greased it all over, and put it away inside a blanket so that it would not dry.

In the morning, quite early, he took his weapons, and taking also his rawhide suit, and the section of the four-fold Bison's intestine which he had filled with blood, he ran into the inlet, and across it, and climbed the mesa near the Shuntekia cliff. When he came within a short distance of the nest of the Eagles, he stopped and slipped on his rawhide suit, and tied the intestine of blood round his neck, like a sausage.

Then he began to cry and shake his head, and he cried louder than there was any need of his doing in reality; for presently the old father of the Eagles, who was away up in the sky, just a mere speck, heard and saw him and came swishing down in a great circle, winding round and round the boy, and the boy looked up and began to cry louder still, as if frightened out of his wits, and finally rolled himself up like a porcupine, and threw himself down into the trail, crying and howling with apparent fear.

The Eagle swooped down on him, and tried to grasp him in his talons, and, kopo kopooo, his claws simply slipped off the rawhide coat.

Then the Eagle made a fiercer grab at him and grew angry, but his claws would continually slip off, until he tore a rent in the intestine about the boy's neck, and the blood began to stream over the boy's coat, making it more slippery than ever.

When the Eagle smelt the blood, he thought he had got him, and it made him fiercer than ever; and finally, during his struggling, he got one talon through a stitch in the coat, and he spread out his wings, and flew up, and circled round and round over the point where the young Eagles nest was, when he let go and shook the boy free, and the boy rolled over and over and came down into the nest; but he struck on a great heap of brush, which broke his fall. He lay there quite still, and the old Eagle swooped down and poised himself on a great crag of rock near by, which was his usual perching place. "There, my children, my little ones," said he, "I have brought you food. Feast yourselves! Feast yourselves! For that reason, I brought it."

So the little Eagles, who were very awkward, long-legged and short-winged, limped tip to the boy and reached out their claws and opened their beaks, ready to strike him in the face. He lay there quite still until they got very near, and then said to them: "Shhsht!" And they tumbled back, being awkward little fellows, and stretched up their necks and looked at him, as Eagles will.

Then the old Eagle said: "Why don't you eat him? Feast yourselves, my children, feast yourselves!"

So they advanced again, more cautiously this time, and a little more determinedly too; and they reached out their beaks to tear him, and he said "Shhsht!" and, under his breath, "Don't eat me! And they jumped back again.

"What in the world is the matter with you little fools?" said the old Eagle. "Eat him! I can't stay here any longer; I have to go away and hunt to feed you; but you don't seem to appreciate my efforts much." And he lifted his wings, rose into the air, and sailed off to the northward.

Then the two young Eagles began to walk around the boy, and to examine him at all points. Finally, they approached his feet and hands.

"Be careful, be careful, don't eat me! Tell me about what time your mother comes home," said he, sitting up. "What time does she usually come?

"Well," said the little Eagles, "she comes home when the clouds begin to gather and throw their shadow over our nest." (Really, it was the shadow of the mother Eagle herself that was thrown over the nest.)

"Very well," said the boy; "what time does your father come home?"

"When the fine rain begins to fall," said they, meaning the dew.

"Oh," said the boy. So, he sat there, and by-and-by, sure enough, away off in the sky, carrying something dangling from her feet, came the old mother Eagle. She soared round and round until she was over the nest, when she dropped her burden, and over and over it fell and tumbled into the nest, a poor, dead, beautiful maiden. The young boy looked at her, and his heart grew very hot, and when the old Eagle came and perched, in a moment he let fly an arrow, and struck her down and dashed her brains out.

"Ha, ha!" exclaimed the boy. "What you have done to many, thus unto you." Then he took his station again, and by-and-by the old father Eagle came, bearing a youth, fair to look upon, and dropped him into the nest. The young boy shut his teeth, and he said: "Thus unto many you have done, and thus unto me you would have done; so unto you." And he drew an arrow and shot him. Then he turned to the two young Eagles and killed them, and plucked out all the beautiful colored feathers about their necks, until he had a large bundle of fine plumes with which he thought to wing his arrows or to waft his prayers.

Then he looked down the cliff and saw there was no way to climb down, and there was no way to climb up. Then he began to cry, and sat on the edge of the cliff, and cried so loud that the old Bat Woman, who was gathering cactus-berries below, or thought she was, overheard the boy.

Said she: "Now, just listen to that. I warrant it is my fool of a grandson, who is always trying to get himself into a scrape. I am sure it must be so. Phoo! phoo!"

She spilled out all the berries she had found from the basket she had on her back, and then labored up to where she could look over the edge of the shelf.

"Yes, there you are," said she; "you simpleton! you wretched boy! What are you doing here?"

"Oh, my grandmother," said he, "I have got into a place and I cannot get out."

"Yes," said she; "if you were anything else but such a fool of a grandson and such a bard-hearted wretch of a boy, I would help you get down; but you never do as your mother and grandmother or grandfathers tell you."

"Ah, my grandmother, I will do just as you tell me this time," said the boy.

"Now, will you?" said she. "Now, can you be certain? -- will you promise me that you will keep your eyes shut, and join me, at least in your heart, in the prayer which I sing when I fly down? Yan lehalliah kiana. Never open your eyes; if you do, the gods will teach you a lesson, and your poor old grandmother, too."

"I will do just as you tell me," said he, as he reached over and took up his plumes and held them ready.

"Not so fast, my child," said she; "you must promise me."

"Oh, my grandmother, I will do just as you tell me," said he.

"Well, step into my basket, very carefully now. As I go down, I shall go very prayerfully, depending on the gods to carry so much more than I usually carry. Do you not wink once, my grandson."

"All right; I will keep my eyes shut this time," said he. So he sat down and squeezed his eyes together, and held his plumes tight, and then the old grandmother launched herself forth on her skin wings. After she had struggled a little, she began to sing "Ha ash tchaa ni,--Ha ash tchaa ni: Tche pa naa,--thlen-thle. Thlen! Thlen! Thlen!

Now, just listen to that," said the boy; "my old grandmother is singing one of those tedious prayers; it will take us forever to go down."

Then presently the old Bat Woman, perfectly unconscious of his state of mind, began to sing again

"Thlen thla kia yai na kia."

"There she goes again," said he to himself; "I declare, I must look up; it will drive me wild to sit here all this time and hear my old grandmother try to sing."

Then, after a little while, she commenced again:

"Ha ash tchaa ni,--Ha ash tchaa ni; Tche pa naa,--thlen-thle. Thlen! Thlen! Thlen!"

The boy stretched himself up, and said: "Look here, grandmother! I have heard your 'Thlen! Thlen! Thlen!' enough this time. I am going to open my eyes.

"Oh, my grandchild, never think of such a thing." Then she began again to sing:

Ha ash tchaa ni,--Ha ash tchaa ni: Tche pa naa,--thlen-thle. Thlen! Thlen! Thlen

She was not near the ground when she finished it the fourth time, and the boy would not stand it any more.

Lo! he opened his eyes, and the old grandmother knew it in a moment. Over and over, boy over bat, bat over boy, and the basket between them, they went whirling and pitching down, the old grandmother tugging at her basket and scolding the boy.

"Now, you foolish, disobedient one! I told you what would happen! You see what you have done!" and so on until they fell to the ground. It fairly knocked the breath out of the boy, and when he got up again, he yelled lustily.

The old grandmother picked herself up, stretched herself, and cried out anew: "You wretched, foolish, hard-hearted boy; I never will do anything for you again-never, never, never!"

"I know, my grandmother," said the boy, "but you kept up that 'Thlen! Thlen! Thlen!' so much. What in the world did you want to spend so much time thlening, thlening; and buzzing round in that way for?"

"Ah, me!" said she, "he never did know anything--never will be taught to know anything."

"Now," said she to him, "you might as well come and eat with me. I have been gathering cactus-fruit, and you can eat and then go home." She took him to the place where she had poured out the contents of the basket, but there was scarcely a cactus-berry. There were cedar-berries, cones, sticks, little balls of dirt, coyote-berries, and everything else uneatable.

"Sit down, my grandson, and eat; strengthen yourself after your various adventures and exertions. I feel very weary myself," said she. And she took a nip of one of them; but the boy couldn't exactly bring himself to eat. The truth is, the old woman's eyes were bad, in the same way that bats' eyes are usually bad, and she couldn't tell a cactus-berry from anything else round and rough.

"Well, inasmuch as you won't eat, my grandson," said she, "why, I can't conceive, for these are very good, it seems to me. You had better run along home now, or your mother will be killing herself thinking of you. Now, I have only one direction to give you. You don't deserve any, but I will give you one. See that you pay attention to it. If not, the worst is your own. You have gathered a beautiful store of feathers. Now, be very careful. Those creatures who bore those feathers have gained their lives from the lives of living beings, and therefore their feathers differ from other feathers. Heed what I say, my grandson.

When you come to any place where flowers are blooming, --where the sunflowers make the field yellow, --walk round those flowers if you want to get home with these feathers. And when you come to more flowers, walk round them. If you do not do that, just as you came you will go back to your home."

"All right, my grandmother," said the boy. So, after bidding her good-by, he trudged away with his bundle of feathers; and when he came to a great plain of sunflowers and other flowers, he walked round them; and when he came to another large patch he walked round them, and then another, and so on; but finally, he stopped, for it seemed to him that there were nothing but fields of flowers all the way home. He thought he had never seen so many before.

"I declare," said he, "I will not walk round those flowers any more. I will hang on to these feathers, though."

So, he took a good hold of them and walked in amongst the flowers. But no sooner had he entered the field than flutter, flutter, flutter, little wings began to fly out from the bundle of feathers, and the bundle began to grow smaller and smaller, until it wholly disappeared.

These wings which flew out were the wings of the Sacred Birds of Summerland, made living by the lives that had supported the birds which bore those feathers, and by coming into the environment which they had so loved, the atmosphere which flowers always bring of summer.

Thus, it was, my children, in the days of the ancients, and for that reason we have little jay-birds, little sparrows, little finches, little willow-birds, and all the beautiful little birds that bring the summer, and they always hover over flowers.

"My friends" [said the story-teller], "that is the way we live. I am very glad, otherwise I would not have told the story, for it is not exactly right that I should, --I am very glad to demonstrate to you that we also have books; only they are not books with marks in them, but words in our hearts, which have been placed there by our ancients long ago, even so long ago as when the world was new and young, like unripe fruit. And I like you to know these things, because people say that the Zuñis are dark people."

Thus shortens my story.

Bear Legend

Cherokee Legend

In the long ago time, there was a Cherokee Clan call the Ani-Tsa-gu-hi (Ahnee-Jah-goo-hee), and in one family of this clan was a boy who used to leave home and be gone all day in the mountains. After a while he went oftener and stayed longer, until at last he would not eat in the house at all, but started off at daybreak and did not come back until night. His parents scolded, but that did no good, and the boy still went every day until they noticed that long brown hair was beginning to grow out all over his body. Then they wondered and asked him why it was that he wanted to be so much in the woods that he would not even eat at home.

Said the boy, "I find plenty to eat there, and it is better than the corn and beans we have in the settlements, and pretty soon I am going into the woods to say all the time." His parents were worried and begged him not leave them, but he said, "It is better there than here, and you see I am beginning to be different already, so that I can not live here any longer. If you will come with me, there is plenty for all of us and you will never have to work for it; but if you want to come, you must first fast seven days."

The father and mother talked it over and then told the headmen of the clan. They held a council about the matter and after everything had been said they decided: "Here we must work hard and have not always enough. There he says is always plenty without work. We will go with him." So they fasted seven days, and on the seventh morning al the Ani-Tsa-gu-hi left the settlement and started for the mountains as the boy led the way.

When the people of the other towns heard of it they were very sorry and sent their headmen to persuade the Ani Tsaguhi to stay at home and not go into the woods to live. The messengers found them already on the way, and were surprised to notice that their bodies were beginning to be covered with hair like that of animals, because for seven days they had not taken human food and their nature was changing. The Ani Tsaguhi would not come back, but said, "We are going where there is always plenty to eat. Hereafter we shall be called Yonv(a) (bears), and when you yourselves are hungry come into the woods and call us and we shall come to give you our own flesh. You need not be afraid to kill us, for we shall live always." Then they taught the messengers the songs with which to call them and bear hunters have these songs still. When they had finished the songs, the Ani Tsaguhi started on again and the messengers turned back to the settlements, but after going a little way they looked back and saw a drove of bears going into the woods.

Aho! We are all related!

Creation of Man

Miwok Legend
Katharine Berry Judson, Myths and Legends of California and the Old Southwest, 1912

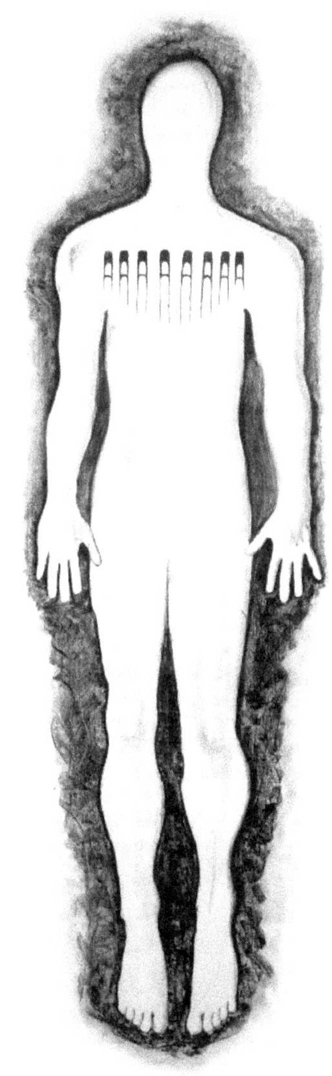

After Coyote had completed making the world, he began to think about creating man. He called a council of all the animals. The animals sat in a circle, just as the Indians do, with Lion at the head, in an open space in the forest.

On Lion's right was Grizzly Bear; next Cinnamon Bear; and so on to Mouse, who sat at Lion's left.

Lion spoke first. Lion said he wished man to have a terrible voice, like himself, so that he could frighten all animals. He wanted man also to be well covered with hair, with fangs in his claws, and very strong teeth.

Grizzly Bear laughed. He said it was ridiculous for any one to have such a voice as Lion, because when he roared, he frightened away the very prey for which he was searching. But he said man should have very great strength; that he should move silently, but very swiftly; and he should be able to seize his prey without noise.

Buck said man would look foolish without antlers. And a terrible voice was absurd, but man should have ears like a spider's web, and eyes like fire.

Mountain Sheep said the branching antlers would bother man if he got caught in a thicket. If man had horns rolled up, so that they were like a stone on each side of his head, it would give his head weight enough to butt very hard.

When it came Coyote's turn, he said the other animals were foolish because they each wanted man to be just like themselves. Coyote was sure he could make a man who would look better than Coyote himself, or any other animal. Of course, he would have to have four legs, with five fingers. Man should have a strong voice, but he need not roar all the time with it.

And he should have feet nearly like Grizzly Bear's, because he could then stand erect when he needed to.

Grizzly Bear had no tail, and man should not have any. The eyes and ears of Buck were good, and perhaps man should have those.

Then there was Fish, which had no hair, and hair was a burden much of the year. So, Coyote thought man should not wear fur. And his claws should be as long as the Eagle's, so that he could hold things in them. But no animal was as cunning and crafty as Coyote, so man should have the wit of Coyote.

Then Beaver talked. Beaver said man would have to have a tail, but it should be broad and flat, so he could haul mud and sand on it. Not a furry tail, because they were troublesome on account of fleas.

Owl said man would be useless without wings.

But Mole said wings would be folly. Man would be sure to bump against the sky. Besides, if he had wings and eyes both, he would get his eyes burned out by flying too near the sun. But without eyes, he could burrow in the soft, cool earth where he could be happy.

Mouse said man needed eyes so he could see what he was eating. And nobody wanted to burrow in the damp earth. So the council broke up in a quarrel.

Then every animal set to work to make a man according to his own ideas. Each one took a lump of earth and modeled it just like himself. All but Coyote, for Coyote began to make the kind of man he had talked of in the council.

It was late when the animals stopped work and fell asleep. All but Coyote, for Coyote was the cunningest of all the animals, and he stayed awake until he had finished his model. He worked hard all night.

When the other animals were fast asleep, he threw water on the lumps of earth, and so spoiled the models of the other animals. But in the morning, he finished his own, and gave it life long before the others could finish theirs. Thus, man was made by Coyote.

The Origin of Yosemite

Long, long ago before the white man came to the West, a large happy tribe of peaceful Indians lived among the trees of beautiful Oak Canyon. This spectacular place is now known as Yosemite Valley, situated in Yosemite National Park, California.

In the beginning these peaceful Indians were called Ah-wah-nees, meaning "Deep Grass Valley," which was the first name given to Yosemite Valley.

It is of interest to note that because of a printer's error at a later date, the spelling of the tribe's name was inadvertently changed to Yosemite. Now Yosemite National Park identifies the original home of the Ah-wah-nee band (Yosemite), southern division of the Miwok Tribe.

Today, the California State flag carries a picture of the grizzly bear as a reminder of the State's official animal, Yo Semitee.

Ah-wah-nees were proud of their Chief, a tall and young athletic man. Early one spring morning, he started off with his spears in hand to hunt for trout in the nearby lake known as Sleeping Water.

Imagine his astonishment when he rounded a large boulder and came face to face with an enormous grizzly bear, probably just out of its winter hibernation!

Such an unexpected meeting caused both of them to rear back in stunned surprise. Immediately, however, all of the fighting spirit within each arose. They attacked one another furiously! The Chief realized his fighting power was not equal to the great strength of the grizzly.

"What can I do to help myself?" he wondered.

At that moment, he saw an oak limb within reach and grabbed it for a weapon.

"I must do everything possible to subdue this bear, even if it means my own death," he thought while he fought. "I am determined that future Ah-wah-nee children will always remember the proud and brave blood that flowed in the veins of their ancestors."

He pounded heavy blows, one after another, upon the head of the grizzly bear. In return, the young Chief received innumerable cuts from the bear's teeth and claws. They exchanged blows that could have been death blows to either one, if each had not been determined to survive. The grizzly bear's hunger drove him to attack; the Chief's pride, courage, and great height strengthened his defense.

On and on they fought. Then when the Chief saw the eyes of the bear glaze with a cold stare, he knew his great moment had come. With his club raised overhead, the Chief brought down a whopping smash upon the head of the bear, who then slowly slumped to the ground. The Chief charged in to finish the task, making sure the grizzly bear was dead.

Exhausted, the young Chief withdrew a short way to rest, but kept his eyes upon the grizzly bear in case it revived. After some time, when he was certain of the bear's death, the Chief stepped forward and skinned the animal.

Later, dragging the bearskin behind him, the Chief returned to his village and proclaimed his victory. Young and old braves gathered to welcome him and to praise his success. The young braves took off, following the trail where the bearskin dragged upon the ground. They found the grizzly bear before any other wild animal had a chance to claim it. Immediately, they set to work and butchered the bear and then carried the parts back to their camp.

In the meantime, the braves prepared a huge fire and sent young runners to the outlying camps, inviting all the people to an evening of feasting.

The victory of their young Chief over the enormous grizzly bear astounded all of the Ah-wah-nees. They cheered and cheered their admiration for their great Chief. They renamed their hero, Chief Yo Semitee, which means "Grizzly Bear."

Following the feast, the entire tribe gathered for a victory dance, attired in all their fine beads and fine feathers. Chief Yo Semitee sat and overlooked the celebration, smoking the peace pipe with his tribal council. More feasting and dancing continued most of the night, as Ah-wah-nees showed their affection for their young and strong Chief.

Yo Semitee's children, and finally all of the tribe, became known as Yo Semitees in honor of their brave Chief.

The Bear Clan

This clan had gone south from the sipahpuni. They had with them the A'ototo Katcina. They soon found the Young Corn Ear (Pihk'ash) people with the Aholi Katcina, who wanted to join them. So the Bear clan chief took them along. They stopped at a place and here had a good crop because they had the two Katcinas with them. The next year they came to a clear stream. In all they stopped ten times before arriving at the Americans, where the sun rises. Here they stopped four years. Their children learned a little English. The land being scarce, the Americans told them to go west and hunt land for themselves, and if anybody would be bad to them (nukpana) and cause their children to die, they (the Americans) would come and cut the Nukapana's heads off. This was told them, because they (the Americans) had been told that down in the old home there had been Popwaktu (sorcerers, etc.). So, they traveled westward, found the Pueblo, but no good land that they could get. So they finally arrived at Shongopavi, where some people lived, and there they settled down.

One time the people saw that the chief, Machito, held a sweet corn-ear between every two fingers, at the same time eating from the other hand. Corn was very scarce at that time, so the people spoke to him about his greediness, at which he got angry and left, taking with him the A'ototo and Aholi. Hunters later found them at a rock, now Bean Spreading Place (Bahpu-Moyanpi), where there is still a stone on which there is some writing called Machitutubeni. Machito left his wife at Shongopavi, also his people, who then formed the Shongopavi Bear clan. When the hunters found him they informed the people at Shongopavi.

Some went there to get them back, but Machito would not listen to them. Then his wife went to him but he would not listen to her either. So, they left him. Machito took a big stone and went with them for some distance to make the landmark between Oraibi and Shongopavi. The people said several times: "Put it here." But he would not listen until arriving at a place called "Ocapchomo," where he placed it, thus making a landmark between the fields of the Shongopavi and his own.

Then Machito and the two Katcinas went up the Oraibi mesa where they remained. Later the Spider people arrived. Machito asked about their wanderings and they told him. He wanted to know why the corn would not grow although they had the Flute cult. The Spider clan chief accused the "North Old Man." Machito then said: "All right, you may live here, but as your cult does not seem to be effective, you watch the sun for me, and when he has arrived at his south limit, you tell me, and we shall have the Soyal ceremony. Also, your pu'htavi does not seem to have been good, so I want you to make my kind of pu'htavi."

After the matter had been settled between Machito and the Spider clan chief, the latter's people came up. Among these were also the Lizard clan, to which the Sand clan is related. These names were given to people while wandering. One would find and see something, perhaps under peculiar circumstances, and he called after it. The Lizard people were also asked what they knew and when they said the

Marau cult, they were also permitted to stay, but were requested to co-operate in the Soyal ceremony. For that reason, Pungnanomsi, who is of the Bear clan, and village chief, now makes the puhu (road) in the night of the Marau ceremony from the natsi at the south end of the kiva towards the rising sun.

The Rattle-snake (Tcu'a) clan also came with the Spider clan to Oraibi, but it is not known how or where this clan became a part of the Spider clan, The Badger people understand medicines, hence they prepare the medicine--for instance, charm liquid--for the Flute, Snake, Marau, and other ceremonies.

Another Badger clan and the Butterfly (Powul) came from Kishi-wuu. These brought the Powamu and Katcina cult.

The Divided Spring (Batki) clan came from where the sun rises.

They came to the village of Oraibi and arranged a contest at Muyiovatki where each planted corn, the Blue Flutes sweet corn, the others, Wupakao, over which they played the whole day. The sweet corn grew first, and so the Blue Flutes to this day go to the village in processions, etc., first closing the well (batni) on the plaza. Later the Drab Flutes (Masitalentu) had to throw their meal, mollas, etc., from a distance to the warrior (Kelehtaka) of the Cakwalalentu, who put them into the well in the booth for them.

The Wanderings of the Bear Clan

Hopi Legend
H. R. Voth, The Traditions of the Hopi, Field Columbian Museum Anthropological Series, 1905

After we had left the sípahpuni the Bear people separated and went ahead of the others. First, they came somewhere near the present site of Phoenix, and stayed there awhile.

They remained for or shorter or longer periods at many different places. Finally, they came to the Little Colorado River, and about there it was where they assumed the clan name, but just exactly where the place was nobody can tell. Their forefathers say that the party once came upon a dead bear that they looked at, and from that they were called forever afterwards the Bear clan. Another party that traveled with them took the hide of the bear, of which the hair had already been removed by little animals (Mû'yi. Pl. Mû'mutyu), who use hair or wool for their nests or burrows.

These people took the skin and cut from it carrying straps (piqö'sha), from which they were called Piqö'sha clan. Another party came upon the bear at just this time and were called Mû'yi clan, after the small mice mentioned before. These three clans arrived there just about the same time, and hence are considered as closely related to one another.

Shortly after another party passed by and found many bluebirds sitting upon the cadaver eating from it; so they were called the Bluebird clan (Chórzh-ñamu). Still later another party, came upon the scene and found the remains of the cadaver full of spider web, so this party was called Spider (Kóhk'ang) clan. By and by a sixth migrating party came along.

By this time the bones of the bear were bleached already. They took the skull, tied yucca leaves to it and carried it along as a drinking vessel in the manner in which the chief's or priest's jugs (móngwikurus) are carried at the present time, and from this. that party was called the jug (Wíkurzh) clan. Finally a seventh party came along and found the place where the bear had been killed swarming with ants, so they were called the Ant (Ánñamu) clan.

These seven clans have derived their names from the same origin, and are now considered as being related to one another. The Bear clan is also said to have halted at various places along the Little Colorado River. From there they moved eastward, stopping for some time at a place called Badger Spring (Honánva).

From this place they again moved eastward, stopped at a place called Mákwutavi, and from here they finally moved to Matö'ví, a large spring a number of miles south of Shongópavi. At this place they also remained for a considerable length of time, but finally they moved northward to the present site of Shongópavi, where they remained. They being the first to arrive at this place, they have ever since considered themselves to be the leading clan in the village, the village chief having also been chosen from their clan.

A few persons of the Bear clan moved from here to Oraíbi, where the chieftainship of the so-called Liberal or Friendly faction is still held by that clan, the Conservative or Hostile faction of that village selecting their chief from the Spider clan. Two of this clan moved to the villages of Shupaúlavi and Mishóngnovi, where the office of the village chief has also remained in this clan to the present day.

How Po'okong Killed the Bear

Told by Lomavantiwa (Shupaulavi)

Mishongnovi they were living, and a bear used to kill the people. At the Skeleton Katcina house lived the Po'okong with his grandmother, and the bear was killing the people. If some one went to his field he was killed. The chief was unhappy over it and was thinking about it. He was thinking about sending Po'okong after it, and for this now the time had arrived. And now he made a bow for the Po'okong of hard wood, and he made arrows and put parrot feathers on the arrows, and on one of the arrows he put blue-bird feathers. He also made a ball that he cut from a buckskin. He sewed it and put cotton into it and then tied it up tightly.

He made one of them and rubbed red ochre (cuta) on it, and for the grandmother he made one baho.

When he was done he brought this to the house of the Po'okong.

The grandmother asked: "What are you doing?" "Yes," he said, "when these, my children, are killed by a bear I am not happy."

"Hao," she said to him, and now the chief said: "Yes, hence I have brought this for you," and then he handed it to the grandmother. She was happy. "Thanks," she said, "thanks." Then he said to the Po'okong: "With this you kill the bear, because I have made this for you;" whereupon he gave the ball, the bow and arrows, and the ball stick to the Po'okong. "Thanks, thanks," the Po'okong said, and was happy. Now he went to hunt the bear. The bear was just going around to hunt for some one, and the Po'okong was also going about in that way, and sure enough, something came to him, running. Now it stood up, holding up the paws. Now the Po'okong being seated, aimed. "Haha (very well)," the bear had now about arrived, but when he had not yet quite arrived, the Po'okong shot and hit him in the throat. When he had shot the bear fell, and now he hit him with the ball stick, and the bear died.

He then skinned him, the legs first, but he did not cut the abdomen. He left the skin in the form of a bag, pulling it over his head like a shirt, but from the feet he cut off the claws. Now he filled it up tightly with dry grass. When he was done, he had made something like a bear. Oh! it was like an ugly bear. Now he tied a woollen rope around his neck. Then he tied it to himself and dragging it ran very fast, screaming: "Uhu, a bear is following me," as he ran. Now the people saw it. Sure enough, a bear came following somebody, and he had almost caught him. "Why, he is following the Po'okong," the people said, and then they ran. Now they told the grandmother, "A bear is following your grandchild." Now alas! the grandmother ran away crying, and went into her kiva.

The Po'okong ascended to the house and threw the bear to the grandmother. The grandmother now, because she was so seared, died at once. The Po'okong laughed at the grandmother and kicked her. "Get up," he said to her, and the grandmother woke up. When she sat up she whipped her grandchild hard. "You are naughty, you have scared me," she said to him; but he had been dragging something dead. The chief was very happy because he heard that he had killed him. From that time the bear stopped. After that he killed no more people. So after that it was better.

The Fourfooted Tribes

Cherokee Legend
Myths of the Cherokee, James Mooney, 1900

In Cherokee mythology, as in that of Indian tribes generally, there is no essential difference between men and animals. In the primal genesis period, they seem to be completely undifferentiated, and we find all creatures alike living and working together in harmony and mutual helpfulness until man, by his aggressiveness and disregard for the rights of the others, provokes their hostility, when insects, birds, fishes, reptiles, and fourfooted beasts join forces against. Henceforth their lives are apart, but the difference is always one of degree only. The animals, like the people, are organized into tribes and have like them their chiefs and townhouses, their councils and ballplays, and the same hereafter in the Darkening land of Us'ûñhi'yï. Man is still the paramount power, and hunts and slaughters the others as his own necessities compel, but is obliged to satisfy the animal tribes in every instance, very much as a murder is compounded for, according to the Indian system, by "covering the bones of the dead" with presents for the bereaved relatives.

This pardon to the hunter is made the easier through a peculiar doctrine of reincarnation, according to which, as explained by the shamans, there is assigned to every animal a definite life term which can not be curtailed by violent means. If it is killed before the expiration of the allotted time the death is only temporary and the body is immediately resurrected in its proper shape from the blood drops, and the animal continues its existence until the end of the predestined period, when the body is finally dissolved and the liberated spirit goes to join its kindred shades in the Darkening land. This idea appears in the story of the bear man and in the belief concerning the Little Deer. Death is thus but a temporary accident and the killing a mere minor crime. By some priests it is held that there are seven successive reanimations before the final end.

Certain supernatural personages, Kana'tĭ and Tsul`kălû' (see the myths), have dominion over the animals, and are therefore regarded as the distinctive gods of the hunter. Kana'tĭ at one time kept the game animals, as well as the pestiferous insects, shut up in a cave underground, from which they were released by his undutiful sons. The primeval animals-the actors in the animal myths and the predecessors of the existing species-are believed to have been much larger, stronger, and cleverer than their successors of the present day. In these myths we find the Indian explanation of certain peculiarities of form, color, or habit, and the various animals are always consistently represented as acting in accordance with their well-known characteristics.

First and most prominent in the animal myths is the Rabbit (*Tsistu*), who figures always as a trickster and deceiver, generally malicious, but often beaten at his own game by those whom he had intended to victimize. The connection of the rabbit with the dawn god and the relation of the Indian myths to the stories current among the southern negroes are discussed in another place. Ball players while in training are forbidden to eat the flesh of the rabbit, because this animal so easily becomes confused in running. On the other hand, their spies seek opportunity to strew along the path which must be taken by their rivals a soup made of rabbit hamstrings, with the purpose of rendering them timorous in action. I

In a ball game between the birds and the fourfooted animals (see story) the Bat, which took sides with the birds, is said to have won the victory for his party by his superior dodging abilities. For this reason, the wings or sometimes the stuffed skin of the bat are tied to the implements used in the game to ensure success for the players. According to the same myth the Flying Squirrel (*Tewa*) also aided in securing the victory, and hence both these animals are still invoked by the ball player. The meat of the common gray squirrel (*sälâ'lï*) is forbidden to rheumatic patients, on account of the squirrel's habit of assuming a cramped position when eating. The stripes upon the back of the ground squirrel (*kiyu`ga*) are the mark of scratches made by the angry animals at a memorable council in which he took it upon himself to say a good word for the archenemy, Man (see "Origin of Disease and Medicine"). The peculiarities of the mink (sûñgï) are accounted for by another story.

The buffalo, the largest game animal of America, was hunted in the southern Allegheny region until almost the close of the last century, the particular species being probably that known in the West as the wood or mountain buffalo. The name in use among the principal gulf tribes was practically the same, and can not be analyzed, viz, Cherokee, *yûñsû'*; Hichitee, *ya'nasi*; Creek, *yëna'sa*; Choctaw, *yanash*. Although the flesh of the buffalo was eaten, its skin dressed for blankets and bed coverings, its long hair woven into belts, and its horns carved into spoons, it is yet strangely absent from Cherokee folklore.

So far as is known it is mentioned in but a single one of the sacred formulas, in which a person under treatment for rheumatism is forbidden to eat the meat, touch the skin, or use a spoon made from the horn of the buffalo, upon the ground of an occult connection between the habitual cramped attitude of a rheumatic and the natural "hump" of that animal.

The elk is known, probably by report, under the name of *a`wï e'gwa*, "great deer", but there is no myth or folklore in connection with it.

The deer, *a`wï'*, which is still common in the mountains, was the principal dependence of the Cherokee hunter, and is consequently prominent in myth, folklore, and ceremonial. One of the seven gentes of the tribe is named from it (Ani'-Kawï', "Deer People"). According to a myth given elsewhere, the deer won his horns in a successful race with the rabbit. Rheumatism is usually ascribed to the work of revengeful deer ghosts, which the hunter has neglected to placate, while on the other hand the aid of the deer is invoked against frostbite, as its feet are believed to be immune from injury by frost. The wolf, the fox, and the opossum are also invoked for this purpose, and for the same reason. When the redroot (*Ceanothus americanus*) puts forth its leaves the people say the young fawns are then in the mountains. On killing a deer, the hunter always cuts out the hamstring from the hind quarter and throws it away, for fear that if he ate it he would thereafter tire easily in traveling.

The powerful chief of the deer tribe is the A`wï' Usdi', or "Little Deer," who is invisible to all except the greatest masters of the hunting secrets, and can be wounded only by the hunter who has supplemented years of occult study with frequent fasts and lonely vigils. The Little Deer keeps constant protecting watch over his subjects, and sees well to it that not one is ever killed in wantonness. When a deer is shot by the hunter the Little Deer knows it at once and is instantly at the spot. Bending low his head he asks of the blood stains upon the ground if they have heard--i.e., if the hunter has asked pardon for the life that he has taken. If the formulistic prayer has been made, all is well, because the necessary sacrifice has been atoned for; but if otherwise, the Little Deer tracks the hunter to his house by the blood drops along the trail, and, unseen and unsuspected, puts into his body the spirit of rheumatism that shall rack him with aches and pains from that time henceforth. As seen at rare intervals--perhaps once in a long lifetime-the Little Deer is pure white and about the size of a small dog, has branching antlers, and is always in company with a large herd of deer. Even though shot by the master hunter, he comes to life again, being immortal, but the fortunate huntsman who can thus make prize of his antlers has in them an unfailing talisman that brings him success in the chase forever after. The smallest portion of one of those horns of the Little Deer, when properly consecrated, attracts the deer to the hunter, and when exposed from the wrapping dazes them so that they forget to run and thus become an easy prey. Like the Ulûñsû'tî stone, it is a dangerous prize when not treated with proper respect, and is--or was--kept always in a secret place away from the house to guard against sacrilegious handling.

Somewhat similar talismanic power attached to the down from the young antler of the deer when properly consecrated. So firm was the belief that it had influence over "anything about a deer" that eighty and a hundred years ago even white traders used to bargain with the Indians for such charms in order to increase their store of deerskins by drawing the trade to themselves. The faith in the existence of the miraculous Little Deer is almost as strong and universal to-day among the older Cherokee as is the belief in a future life.

The bears (*yânû*) are transformed Cherokee of the old clan of the Ani'-Tsâ'gûhï (see story, "Origin of the Bear"). Their chief is the White Bear, who lives at Kuwâ'hï, "Mulberry place," one of the high peaks of the Great Smoky mountains, near to the enchanted lake of Atagâ'hï, to which the wounded bears go to be cured of their hurts. Under Kuwâ'hï and each of three other peaks in the same mountain region the bears have townhouses, where they congregate and hold dances every fall before retiring to their dens for the winter. Being really human, they can talk if they only would, and once a mother bear was heard singing to her cub in words which the hunter understood. There is one variety known as *kalâs'-gûnâhi'ta*, "long hams," described as a large black bear with long legs and small feet, which is always lean, and which the hunter does not care to shoot, possibly on account of its leanness. It is believed that new-born cubs are hairless, like mice.

The wolf (*wa'`ya*) is revered as the hunter and watchdog of Kana'tï, and the largest gens in the tribe bears the name of Ani'-wa'`ya, "Wolf people." The ordinary Cherokee will never kill one if he can possibly avoid it, but will let the animal go by unharmed, believing that the kindred of a slain wolf will surely revenge his death, and that the weapon with which the deed is done will be rendered worthless for further shooting until cleaned and exercised by a medicine man. Certain persons, however, having knowledge of the proper atonement rites, may kill wolves with impunity, and are hired for this purpose by others who have suffered from raids upon their fish traps or their stock. Like the eagle killer (see "The Bird Tribes"), the professional wolf killer, after killing one of these animals, addresses to it a prayer in which he seeks to turn aside the vengeance of the tribe by laying the burden of blame upon the people of some other settlement. He then unscrews the barrel of his gun and inserts into it seven small sourwood rods heated over the fire, and allows it to remain thus overnight in the running stream; in the morning the rods are taken out and the barrel is thoroughly dried and cleaned.

The dog (*gi`lï'*), although as much a part of Indian life among the Cherokee as in other tribes, hardly appears in folklore. One myth makes him responsible for the milky way; another represents him as driving the wolf from the comfortable house fire and taking the place for himself. He figures also in connection with the deluge. There is no tradition of the introduction of the horse (*sâ'gwälï*, from *asâ'gwälihû'*, from "a pack or burden") or of the cow (*wa'`ka*, from the Spanish, *vaca*). The hog is called, *sïkwä*, this being originally the name of the opossum, which somewhat resembles it in expression, and which is now distinguished as *sïkwä utse'tstï*, "grinning sïkwä". In the same way the sheep, another introduced animal, is called *a`wï' unäde'na*, "woolly deer"; the goat, *a`wï' ahänu'lähï*, "bearded deer," and the mule, "*sâ'gwä'lï digû'lanähi'ta*", "long-eared horse." The cat, also obtained from the whites, is called *wesä*, an attempt at the English "pussy." When it purrs by the fireside, the children say it is counting in Cherokee, "*ta'ladu', nûñ'gï, ta'ladu', nûñ'gï*," "sixtccn, four, sixteen, four." The elephant, which a few of the Cherokee have seen in shows, is called by them *käma'mä u'tänû*, "great butterfly," from the supposed resemblance of its long trunk and flapping ears to the proboscis and wings of that insect. The anatomical peculiarities of the opossum, of both sexes, are the subject of much curious speculation among the Indians, many of whom believe that its young are produced without any help from the male. It occurs in one or two of the minor myths.

The fox (*tsu'`lä*) is mentioned in one of the formulas, but does no appear in the tribal folklore. The black fox is known by a different name (*inâ'lï*). The odor of the skunk (*dïlä'*) is believed to keep off contagious diseases, and the scent bag is therefore taken out and hung over the doorway, a small hole being pierced in it in order that the contents may ooze out upon the timbers. At times, as in the smallpox epidemic of 1866, the entire body of the animal was thus hung up, and in some cases, as an additional safeguard, the meat was cooked and eaten and the oil rubbed over the skin of the person. The underlying idea is that the fetid smell repels the disease spirit, and upon the same principle the buzzard, which is so evidently superior to carrion smells, is held to be powerful against the same diseases.

The beaver (*dâ'yï*), by reason of its well-known gnawing ability, against which even the hardest wood is not proof, is invoked on behalf of young children just getting their permanent teeth. According to the little formula which is familiar to nearly every mother in the tribe, when the loosened milk tooth is pulled out or drops out of itself, the child runs with it around the house, repeating four times, "*Dâ'yï, skïntä'* (Beaver, put a new tooth into my jaw)" after which he throws the tooth upon the roof of the house.

In a characteristic song formula to prevent frostbite the traveler, before starting out on a cold winter morning, rubs his feet in the ashes of the fire and sings a song of four verses, by means of which, according to the Indian idea, he acquires in turn the cold-defying powers of the wolf, deer, fox, and opossum, four animals whose feet, it is held, are never frostbitten. After each verse he imitates the cry and the action of the animal. The words used are archaic in form and may be rendered "I become a real wolf," etc. The song runs:

Tsûñ'wa'`ya-ya' (repeated four times), *wa + a!* (prolonged howl). (Imitates a wolf pawing the ground with his feet.)

Tsûñ'-ka'wi-ye' (repeated four times), *sauh! sauh! sauh! sauh!* (Imitates call and jumping of a deer.)

Tsûñ'-tsu'`la-ya' (repeated four times), *gaih! gaih! gaih! gaih!* (Imitates barking and scratching of a fox.)

Tsûñ'-sï'kwa-ya' (repeated four times), *kï* +. (Imitates the cry of an opossum when cornered, and throws his head back as that animal does when feigning death.)

The Offended Rolling Stone

Pawnee Legend

Dorsey, Publications of the Carnegie Institution, lix, 446, No. 126

Coyote was going along, and as he had not had anything to eat for some time, he was very hungry. In the evening he went to a high hill and sat down. Early the next morning he started again. He came to a big round stone. He took out his knife and said: "Grandfather, this knife I give to you as a present. I want you to help me to get something to eat."

Coyote went over a hill, and there in the bottom was a village of people. He went into the village and he could see meat hanging on poles everywhere in the camp. He went into one of the tipis and the people in the tipi roasted a piece of meat for him. just as he was about to taste of the meat he thought of his knife and said: "Why did I give my knife to that stone? I should have kept it and then I should have been able to cut the meat without having to pull it with my hands." He asked to be excused and went out.

He went to where the stone was. He said: "Grandfather, I will have to take back this knife, for I have found a village of people with plenty of meat." He went over the hills and into the bottom, but there was no village there. Coyote went back and returned the knife to the stone. He went back over the hills and there saw the village and he entered one of the tipis. They placed before him some meat. He began to chew the meat. He thought of his knife. He went back to the stone, and as he took the knife the stone said: "Why do you take the knife away from me? I am now going to kill you."

Then the stone ran after the Coyote. Coyote ran and came to a den of Bears. He told the Bears that a person was running after him and he asked them to help him. The Bears said that they were not afraid of anything. They asked what the thing was, and he said it was the stone. The Bears said: "Keep on running. We can not do anything with the stone." The stone was close to Coyote when he came up to another den of Mountain-Lions. They also told Coyote to pass on, as they could not do anything for him. After a while Coyote came to a Buffalo standing all alone, but when the Buffalo found out that it was the stone running after Coyote, he told him to pass on.

At last Coyote came to a place where the Bull-Bats stayed. Coyote said: "Grandchildren, there is a person running after me." The Bull-Bats then said: "Enter our lodge and remain there." When the stone came rolling up it said: "Where is that person who came here?" The Bull-Bats did not reply and the stone became angry. Then the Bull-Bats said: "He is here and we are going to protect him." The Bull-Bats flew up and then down, and they expelled flatus on the stone. Every time they did this a piece broke off from the stone. The largest Bull-Bat came down and expelled flatus right on the center and broke the stone into pieces. Then the Coyote was told to come out and go on his way.

Coyote started off, and when he got over the hills he turned around and yelled at the Bull-Bats and said: "All you big-nosed funny things, how you did behave to that stone." The Bull-Bats heard it and did not pay any attention, but he kept on making fun of them. Then the Bull-Bats flew up in a group, and came down, and with their wings they got the stones together again and started it to rolling, and said: "Go and kill that fellow." The stone then ran after Coyote and Coyote tried to get away, but he could not. At last he gave out. He jumped over a steep bank and the stone was right behind him. As Coyote struck the bottom, the stone fell on him and killed him. This is why we used to find dead coyotes in the hills and valleys.

The Trickster Kills the Children

Arapaho
Dorsey and Kroeber, Field Museum: Anthropological Series, v, 101, No. 49

Nihansan was travelling down a stream. As he walked along on the bank, he saw something red in the water. They were red plums. He wanted them badly. Taking off his clothes, he dived in and felt over the bottom with his hands; but he could find nothing, and the current carried him down-stream and to the surface again.

He thought. He took stones and tied them to his wrists and ankles so that they should weigh him down in the water. Then he dived again; he felt over the bottom, but could find nothing. When his breath gave out, he tried to come up, but could not. He was nearly dead, when at last the stones on one side fell off and he barely rose to the surface sideways and got a little air. As he revived, floating on his back, he saw the plums hanging on the tree above him. He said to himself: "You fool!" He scolded himself a long time. Then he got up, took off the stones, threw them away, and went and ate the plums. He also filled his robe with them.

Then he went on down the river. He came to a tent. He saw a bear-woman come out and go in again. Going close to the tent, he threw a plum so that it dropped in through the top of the tent. When it fell inside, the bear-women and children all scrambled for it. Then he threw another and another. At last, one of the women said to her child: "Go out and see if that is not your uncle Nihansan." The child went out, came back, and said: "Yes, it is my uncle Nihansan." Then Nihansan came in. He gave them the plums, and said: "I wonder that you never get plums, they grow so near you!" The bear-women wanted to get some at once. He said: "Go up the river a little way; it is not far. Take all your children with you that are old enough to pick. Leave the babies here and I will watch them." They all went.

Then he cut all the babies' heads off. He put the heads back into the cradles; the bodies he put into a large kettle and cooked. When the bear-women came back, he said to them: "Have you never been to that hill here? There were many young wolves there." "In that little hill here?" they asked. "Yes. While you were gone, I dug the young wolves out and cooked them." Then they were all pleased. They sat down and began to eat. One of the children said: "This tastes like my little sister." "Hush!" said her mother, "don't say that." Nihansan became uneasy. "It is too hot here," he said, and took some plums and went off a little distance; there he sat down and ate. When he had finished, he shouted: "Ho! Ho! bear-women, you have eaten your own children."

All the bears ran to their cradles and found only the heads of the children. At once they pursued him. They began to come near him. Nihansan said: "I wish there were a hole that I could hide in." When they had nearly caught him, he came to a hole and threw himself into it.

The hole extended through the hill, and he came out on the other side while the bear-women were still standing before the entrance. He painted himself with white paint to look like a different person, took a willow stick, put feathers on it, and laid it across his arm. Then he went to the women. "What are you crying about?" he asked them. They told him. He said: "I will go into the hole for you," and crawled in. Soon he cried as if hurt, and scratched his shoulders. Then he came out, saying: "Nihansan is too strong for me. Go into the hole yourselves; he is not very far in." They all went in, but soon came out again and said: "We cannot find him."

Nihansan entered once more, scratched himself bloody, bit himself, and cried out. He said: "He has long finger nails with which he scratches me. I cannot drag him out. But he is at the end of the hole. He cannot go back farther. If you go in, you can drag him out. He is only a little farther than you went last time."

They all went into the hole. Nihansan got brush and grass and made a fire at the entrance. "That sounds like flint striking," said one of the women. "The flint birds are flying," Nihansan said. "That sounds like fire," said another woman. "The fire birds are flying about; they will soon be gone by." "That is just like smoke," called a woman. "Thc smoke birds are passing. Go on, he is only a little farther, you will catch him soon," said Nihansan. Then the heat followed the smoke into the hole. The bear-women began to shout. "Now the heat birds are flying," said Nihansan.

Then the bears were all killed. Nihansan put out the fire and dragged them out. "Thus, one obtains food when he is hungry," he said. He cut up the meat, ate some of it, and hung the rest on branches to dry. Then he went to sleep.

The Bungling Host

Thompson
Teit, Memoirs of the American Folk-Lore Society, vi, 40

The Black Bear invited the Coyote to her underground lodge. He went the next morning, and on arriving was kindly treated by the Bear. She gave him berries and other food to eat, which was very acceptable to him, as he was almost famishing.

Before long the Black Bear put more wood on the fire, and placed a dish down by the side of the fire. Then she held her hands, fingers turned downward, in front of the blaze. Before long melted fat commenced to drip from her finger-tips into the dish below, which in a short time became quite full.

She took the dish and placed it in front of the Coyote, asking him to partake of the fat, which he did, eating as much as he was able. After finishing his repast, the Coyote said that he would now go home. At the same time, he invited the Black Bear to his house on the morrow, when he said he would return her dish, which in the mean time he would borrow so as to take home the rest of the fat for his wife.

In due course the Black Bear arrived at the Coyote's house, where she was treated to some offal which the Coyote had found, but which he told her was fresh, as he had been out hunting and had just brought it in. After a while the Coyote told his wife to stir the fire, because he wanted to get some fat to give to his guest.

He then set the dish down close to the fire, and holding up his paws in front of the blaze, exactly as the Black Bear had done, he awaited results. As there was no sign of any fat coming, he placed his paws still nearer to the flame, and held them there until they commenced to shrivel and curl up with the heat, and still there were no signs of any grease dripping down. His paws had now almost shrunk up into a ball. He was unable to endure the pain any longer, withdrew his hands from the fire, and ran around the house, howling with pain.

The Black bear then said to him, "What a fool you are! Poor fellow! Watch me how I do it." She then held up her paws in front of the fire, as she had done on the previous day, and before long the dish was full of grease. She then made the Coyote a present of the grease, and told him never to try and do what was beyond his power.

Sometime afterwards the Coyote felt hungry and thought he would pay a visit to Tsalas, who lived in an underground lodge some little distance away. Upon entering, Tsalas treated him kindly, telling him that he would go and get some fresh fish for him to eat.

He went outside, took a withe from some neighboring bushes, and went down to the river, where he made a small hole in the ice, and commenced to dive for fish. The Coyote, meanwhile, watched all his movements from the top of the ladder. Before long, Tsalas had caught a goodly number of fish, which he strung on the withe, and returning home, cooked some of them for the Coyote, who soon ate his fill.

On leaving, the Coyote invited Tsalas to visit him at his house on the morrow. Accordingly, the next day, Tsalas repaired to the Coyote's house, where he was offered old meat; but, unlike the Black Bear, he was not fond of such food. Therefore, the Coyote proposed to go and get some fresh fish for him. The Coyote left the house, took a withe, and after making a hole in the ice put his head down the hole in order to look for the fish before diving. But in trying to get his head out again he found that he could not.

Wondering at this long absence, Tsalas went to look for his friend, and found him with his head stuck down in the ice-hole. He pulled him out, more dead than alive, and addressing him, said, "Poor fellow! Why should you make yourself worse off than you already are? You are very foolish to try to do things that are beyond your powers. Now look at me!" Tsalas then put his head down in the hole and soon commenced to toss plenty of fish out on the ice. He made a present of them to the Coyote, and went home, leaving the Coyote in anything but a pleasant mood.

Some time afterwards the Coyote went to the mountains to watch the Magpie and learn his methods of hunting. The latter had set a net-snare close by his underground lodge. He went up the mountains, singled out a large buck deer, which he teased, and called names, such as "big posterior," "hairy posterior," "short-tail."

The buck at last grew angry and charged the Magpie, who ran away. He just kept a little ahead of the buck, so as to encourage him, and led him right into the snare, in which his antlers stuck fast, whilst the Magpie jumped over it, and turning round, stabbed the entangled buck to death.

The Coyote made up his mind that he would do as the Magpie had done. So, he placed a net-snare close by his house, and, going up the mountains, soon fell in with a buck deer, whom he commenced to belittle and slander, calling him all kinds of nasty names, just as the Magpie had done. The buck grew angry, charged the Coyote, who made for home, where his snare was, with the buck close after him. On reaching the net, the Coyote tried to jump over it, but failed to do so. He fell into the net and became entangled in it. Then the buck began to prod him with his antlers, and would have killed him if the people had not run out and prevented it by killing the buck.

The Wish to Marry a Star

Timagami Ojibwa
Speck, Memoirs of the Geological Survey of Canada: Anthropological Series, ix, 47

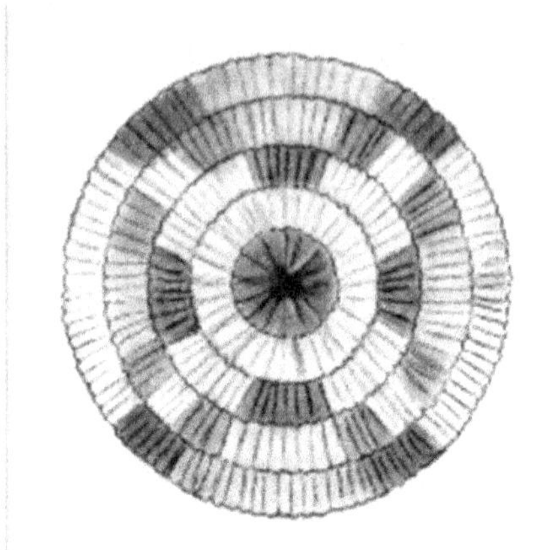

At the time of which my story speaks people were camping just as we are here. In the winter time they used birch bark wigwams. All the animals could then. talk together. Two girls, who were very foolish, talked foolishly and were in no respect like the other girls of their tribe, made their bed out-of-doors, and slept right out under the stars. The very fact that they slept outside during the winter proves how foolish they were.

One of these girls asked the other, "With what star would you like to sleep, the white one or the red one?" The other girl answered, "I'd like to sleep with the red star." "Oh, that's all right," said the first one, "I would like to sleep with the white star. He's the younger; the red is the older." Then the two girls fell asleep. When they awoke, they found themselves in another world, the star world. There were four of them there, the two girls and the two stars who had become men. The white star was very, very old and was grey-headed, while the younger was red-headed. He was the red star. The girls stayed a long time in this star world, and the one who had chosen the white star was very sorry, for he was so old.

There was an old woman up in this world who sat over a hole in the sky, and, whenever she moved, she showed them the hole and said, "That's where you came from." They looked down through and saw their people playing down below, and then the girls grew very sorry and very homesick. One evening, near sunset, the old woman moved a little way from the hole.

The younger girl heard the noise of the *mitewin* down below. When it was almost daylight, the old woman sat over the hole again and the noise of *mitewin* stopped; it was her spirit that made the noise. She was the guardian of the *mitewin.*

One morning the old woman told the girls, "If you want to go down where you came from, we will let you down, but get to work and gather roots to make a string-made rope, twisted. The two of you make coils of rope as high as your heads when you are sitting. Two coils will be enough." The girls worked for days until they had accomplished this. They made plenty of rope and tied it to a big basket. They then got into the basket and the people of the star world lowered them down. They descended right into an Eagle's nest, but the people above thought the girls were on the ground and stopped lowering them. They were obliged to stay in the nest, because they could do nothing to help themselves.

Said one, "We'll have to stay here until some one comes to get us." Bear passed by. The girls cried out, "Bear, come and get us. You are going to get married sometime. Now is your chance!" Bear thought, "They are not very good-looking women." He pretended to climb up and then said, "I can't climb up any further." And he went away, for the girls didn't suit him.

Next came Lynx. The girls cried out again, "Lynx, come up and get us. You will go after women some day!" Lynx answered, "I can't, for I have no claws," and he went away.

Then an ugly-looking man, Wolverine, passed and the girls spoke to him. "Hey, wolverine, come and get us." Wolverine started to climb up, for he thought it a very fortunate thing to have these women and was very glad. When he reached them, they placed their hair ribbons in the nest. Then Wolverine agreed to take one girl at a time, so he took the first one down and went back for the next. Then Wolverine went away with his two wives and enjoyed himself greatly, as he was ugly and nobody else would have him.

They went far into the woods, and then they sat down and began to talk. "Oh!" cried one of the girls, "I forgot my hair ribbon." Then Wolverine said, "I will run back for it." And he started off to get the hair ribbons. Then the girls hid and told the trees, whenever Wolverine should come back and whistle for them, to answer him by whistling. Wolverine soon returned and began to whistle for his wives, and the trees all around him whistled in answer. Wolverine, realizing that he had been tricked, gave up the search and departed very angry.

The Deceived Blind Man

Smith Sound Eskimo

Boas, Journal of American Folk-Lore, xii, 169, No. 7

There was a blind boy (or young man) who lived with his mother and sister. They went to a place where there was no one and lived alone. One day, when they were in their tent, a bear came up to it. Though the boy was blind he had a bow, and the woman aimed it at the bear for him. The arrow struck the bear and killed it.

The mother, however, deceived her son and told him he had missed it. She cut it up and then cooked it. The young man now smelled the bear-meat, and asked his mother whether it was not bear he was smelling. She, however, told him he was mistaken. Then she and her daughter ate it, but she would give him nothing. His sister, however, put half her food in her dress secretly, to give him later. When her mother asked her why she was eating so much (noticing that she seemed to eat an unusual quantity), the girl answered that she was hungry. Later, when her mother was away, she gave the meat to her brother. In this way he discovered that his mother had deceived him. Then he wished for another chance to kill something, when he might not be thus deceived by his mother.

One day, when he was out of doors, a large loon came down to him and told him to sit on its head. The loon then flew with him toward its nest, and finally brought him to it, on a large cliff. After they had reached this, it began to fly again, and took him to a pond. The loon then dived with him, in order to make him recover his eyesight. It would dive and ask him whether he was smothering; when he answered that he was, it took him above the surface to regain his breath. Thus, they dived, until the blind boy could see again. His eyesight was now very strong; he could see as far as the loon, and could even see where his mother was, and what she was doing. Then he returned. When he came back, his mother was afraid, and tried to excuse herself, and treated him with much consideration.

The Maiden who Became a Bear

The Dîné
Origin Myths of the Navaho Indians Aileen O'Bryan

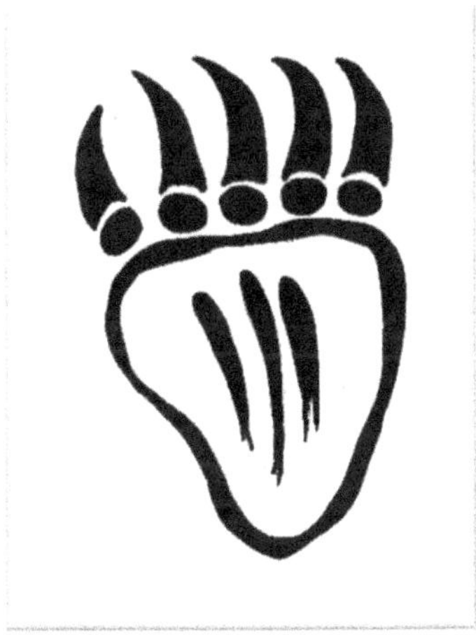

When the brothers returned that night, they entered the house. Not seeing the Coyote among them their sister went out to look for him; not finding him she asked her eldest brother what they had done with her husband. The eldest brother said: "We sent him back with the meat a long time ago. We thought that you would have the meat cooked for us by now." The woman looked straight at her brothers and told them that they had killed the Coyote. The brothers said: "No, sister, we have told you the truth. We sent him back with the meat early in the day." But she accused them four times of killing her husband. Four times they gave the same answer. Then she went to the rainbow path and there she found the meat. From there she tracked the Coyote to the canyon's edge and she found where he had been killed by the Swallow People.

After the woman left her brothers to go look for the Coyote the eldest brother said: "Listen now to my words: our sister is about to do something still more evil."

When the woman returned to the house, she told her brothers that the people in the canyon had killed her husband. She would not sit down in the home. She prepared herself to go against the cliff people. First, she took her sewing awls and sharpened them; then she hid her heart and lungs as the Coyote had taught her, and turned herself into a great bear with sharp teeth and claws, and she went forth against the people of the canyon. When she came among them, they shot at her with their arrows, but they did not harm her. When she returned home, she turned back into her woman form. But every night she went out in her bear form and killed the cliff people with her teeth and claws; however, she did not eat them as a wolf or bear would have done.

It was then that the people moved into the caves in the cliff walls. The Rainbow's strength was their strength. The people, in those days, used a rainbow for their ladder as well as for their bridge. They used it and it was not difficult for them to carry up their goods and to build houses in the caves. For a long time, the people abandoned their homes on the floor of the canyon; but the bear woman followed them. She would dig up through the earth and kill them. After that they built their homes of rock in the caves.

Always when she returned to her brothers, she was in her woman form. But her name was now Esdza'shash nadle, the Woman who Became a Bear.

Soon she went out even during the day to kill people. She became so terrible that the Spider People, the Lizard People, and the Swallow People built high in the sides of the canyons where she could not reach them. After a time, the brothers became frightened. They did not know what to do. But they knew that their turn would come; that she would kill them too. The eldest brother had a plan. He, together with the other brothers, pushed the ashes of the fire to one side and they dug a hole under the fireplace. They hid the youngest brother in this hole which had four sides to hold back the earth. They covered the hole with a slab over which they put earth; they then raked the ashes over it and built a fire. Then they went to the east of their dwelling.

When the Bear Woman returned no one was in the house. She went to relieve herself and said: "Whichever way the water runs, that is the direction my brothers have taken." It showed east; so, she followed in her bear form. She tracked them and she killed the 11 brothers. She saw that the youngest was missing. She returned to the house. Again, she went to relieve herself, and she said: "Whichever way it flows there my brother is." But it neither flowed nor fell. So, she went into the house and tore the rocks out. She found her youngest brother under the firestone.

The Bear Woman spoke kind words to him. "Come out, my brother," she said, "your hair looks dirty; it needs washing and dressing; let me care for it." The little breeze whispered in the boy's ear: "She has killed your 11 brothers, and now she wants your life." The little breeze stayed on the boy's ear and told him to have weapons ready when she began to comb his hair. It told him also, to loosen the string ties of his loin cloth. "She will place you facing the sun when she starts to comb your hair; but you must sit so that. you can see her shadow." The woman made her brother sit facing the sun; but be said: "Sister, the sun is too bright for my eyes." After four times she agreed to let him sit where he chose. He sat where he could watch her shadow. She got the grass brush, which they used for the hair, and she brushed his hair once or twice; and out grew her lips to the shape of a bear's mouth with long teeth. The boy turned and said: "What is it, sister?" She said: "Oh, I am just sleepy." The breeze was now busy in the boy's ear telling him what would happen and what he should do. He was to be saved; but the price paid was the lives of his 11 brothers.

The boy was told that the fourth time that he caught her changing into the form of a bear he must jump up and run as fast as he could to the place where she had hidden her heart and lungs. "About the moment when she is about to catch you, you will jump over a big cactus. She will have to go around it and you will gain ground. The second time you will jump over a big growth of yucca; the third time, over a log; and the fourth time you will jump over a big boulder."

Now the boy watched her shadow, and each time that he caught her changing into the bear form he turned and looked at her and she became the woman. After the fourth time he had his muscles set, and jumped away from her. Sure enough, she grabbed his belt; but the tie loosened. She was near him when he reached the cactus. He jumped over it; she ran around it. The second time she was near him he jumped over the yucca; the third time he jumped over the fallen log; and the fourth time, over the great boulder. Then her heart became nervous, and the chipmunk who was guarding it screamed. The heart and the lungs were beating up and down just ahead of the boy. They were covered with oak leaves. The Bear Woman cried out: "Oh, brother, brother, stop! There are my heart and my lungs. There is my life."

Now when the boy saw the leaves beating up and down in fright, he jumped over them, and he shot his arrow into them. The Bear Woman fell, and the blood gushed out of her mouth and nostrils. The boy returned near her, and the little breeze told him to stop the blood. It must not flow, for if it met the blood from her heart, she would become whole again. So, the boy pulled the Bear Woman's carcass away. He was angry. He spread her legs and cut out her sex organs. He said: "You have the sex organs of a woman, and great trouble has come of it." He tossed it to the top of a tree and said: "The people of the earth shall use you henceforth." It became the pitch that is found on cedar and pinon trees. Then he cut off her breasts and said: "You have a woman's breasts and still you have caused great trouble." He tossed them to the top of a tree and said: "The people of the earth shall use you." And they became pinon nuts.

After these things happened many people planned to leave the mesas. They were afraid of the Woman who became a bear. They buried the Calendar Stone; they wrapped their dead; and leaving their belongings, they went away. But before they left, they drew pictures on the rocks of all the things that trouble came from.

Now only the Swallow People and the Lizard, Snake, and Spider People remained. All the others said that they would never return to make the mesa country their home. They moved into Montezuma Valley and built their homes around Ute Mountain. Their main dwellings were Yucca House and a place near a spring east of Ute Mountain. They multiplied and their homes covered quite a lot of territory. They moved to places where they found good water, good building material, and where their plants would grow. But always they came to where their chief person lived. This was a place west of Dolores called Sage Brush Spring. They moved their chief, or head person of their tribe, there. This person was considered sacred, and kept away from the sun and the light all of the time. Where he lived sacred stones were placed at his feet, at his out-stretched arms and head. Prayer sticks guarded his body. Then bluebird feathers were set around him. Whatever he said was done. They lived for a time at Sage Brush Spring; but corn did not grow well there; living was difficult. They moved to the foot of Elk Mountain.

The Origin of Some Oraibi Clans

Hopi Legends
The Traditions of the Hopi H. R. Voth [1905]

Away down the sípapu in the under-world the people lived in the same manner as they do here. The wife of the chief of the Bear clan often danced in the Butterfly dance (Políhtikivee), at which the chief got angry. The Spider clan had also a chief. The Bear chief sent the Pö'okong to limit for them another life (kátci) or world and see whether they could not get out. He was so angry at his wife's participating in the dance, fearing that she would be led astray, he wanted to go away and leave her.

Pö'okong and his younger brother Balö'ongahoya went in search of another world, and when they returned, reported that there was an opening right above them. Pö'okong had reached it by means of a reed on which he had spit and thus made it strong. The chief said, as they were still dancing (the Butterfly dance) they would move in four days. After four days they were still dancing, and the chief said to some one that he would not tell his wife anything, but try to find another wife.

So, he left, being accompanied by Pö'okong and, Balö'ongahoya, the Pölis still dancing wildly. They started and went out, Pö'okong first, then Balö'ongahoya, then the Bear clan chief, who was followed by the Spider clan chief. Then the Bear clan people, the Spider clan people, and after them many other people came out. When many were out the Bear chief closed the opening.

When they were out the chief said, "Well, what now?" They were in the dark yet, the entrance, however, being closed. The chief sent the Eagle who flew around hunting an opening or light. H returned, and the chief asked: "Taá um hin nawóti?" "Well, I found an opening, and made it more light, but it is very hot high up yet. Send another one."

So, the chief sent the Buzzard (Wicóko). The latter ascended higher but got burned (hence he has no feathers on his head and wings), but he made it lighter, when he returned that chief said: "Thank you. Well, now what? Now it is somewhat better. The sky has been opened somewhat more and it is much lighter." The question arose: Which way? The Bear clan spoke for the South, the Spider clan for the north, and the latter talking more and getting the greater crowd, the Spider clan went northward.

The Hunter and his Dogs (Second Version)

Hitchiti Stories Myths and Tales of the Southeastern Indians John R. Swanton [1929]

A man having many dogs fell sick and lay in a helpless condition. One small puppy was able to talk with his master. Whatever the big dogs thought they told to the puppy and he in turn told his master all that had been said. While they were there the big dogs said to the puppy, "There is no food hereabouts. Tell him we can carry him along with us on a hunt if he agrees." The puppy told his master. He said, "They want me to tell you that we could take you hunting with us." When be told him that, the man answered, "You could not take me in anyway." But the dogs said to the puppy again, "Tell him we know a way by which we can take him if he agrees to go." When he told his master the latter said, "You may take me if you can think of a way." The puppy told the big dogs. "If that is so we will take him with us," said the dogs.

They laid his gun on the bedding, and all seized the corners of the blanket under him, lifted it up and went on with it. When they got far off, they stopped and made a camp, and laid the man down, and the dogs collected wood for him. Then they built a fire and while the man lay still the dogs went out hunting for him. Each evening, when they came back, they brought some squirrels or turkeys they had killed and he ate them. The man lying there got a little better. While he was still in bed, the dogs said to the puppy, "Tell him we will move on again if he agrees." The puppy told his master. He said, "They say it is best to move." When the puppy told him, he said, "All right." So, they seized the blanket again, carried him along, and made another camp. Laying the man down there the dogs went hunting and returned in the evening with some squirrels or some turkeys they had killed or some tortoises they had found. The man ate them in bed and got better. When he got up and could go about for short distances, the dogs went out hunting one morning and he heard them barking not very far from camp. The puppy had remained with the man in camp. Then one dog came back on the run and said, "We have treed a bear but we can't do anything with him. I have come to see if our master can not come to that place, which is only a short distance away." He told this to the little dog, and the puppy told it to his master. "If I go slowly, I may be able to get there," said the man. The puppy said, "He says, 'I will go.'" When he told the other dog, he ran back again and informed the rest. "He is going to come," he said.

So, the dogs waited and kept watch on the bear. When the man and the puppy got there, they brought the man's gun. The man shot down the bear which they had treed, skinned it, and cut it up. Then the dogs seized the pieces thus cut up and carried them all back to camp. They had plenty of meat. "Now I am well," said the man. "Let us go home." He said to the puppy, "Tell the big dogs." The puppy said to the dogs, "He wants me to say to you 'We must go home,'" and the big dogs said, "All right; but tell him when we get there and his former mother-in-law wants to give him something to eat, before he eats, he must let us eat." So, he told his master. "This is what I have been told to say," he said to his master. "All right," he said, and they started on. When they reached his home, his former mother-in-law set out something for him to eat. The man sat down to eat but remembered what the dogs had told him. The thought troubled him very much. He sat without eating. Then he saw the dogs looking at him. The puppy sat looking, and the man sitting there gave a piece of bread to each. The puppy took the bread, moved away, and sat down. As he sat crying, he fell over and died. All of the dogs sat down with their bread in the same way, cried, and died. It is said that all of them died.

This is how it is told.

The Rabbit and the Bear with the Flint Body

Myths and Legends of the Sioux McLaughlin, Marie L. (1916)

The Rabbit and his grandmother were in dire straits, because the rabbit was out of arrows. The fall hunt would soon be on and his quiver was all but empty. Arrow sticks he could cut in plenty, but he had nothing with which to make arrowheads.

"You must make some flint arrowheads," said his grandmother. "Then you will be able to kill game."

"Where shall I get the flint?" asked the rabbit.

"From the old bear chief," said his old grandmother. For at that time all the flint in the world was in the bear's body.

So, the rabbit set out for the village of the Bears. It was winter time and the lodges of the bears were set under the shelter of a hill where the cold wind would not blow on them and where they had shelter among the trees and bushes.

He came at one end of the village to a hut where lived an old woman. He pushed open the door and entered. Everybody who came for flint always stopped there because it was the first lodge on the edge of the village. Strangers were therefore not unusual in the old woman's hut, and she welcomed the rabbit. She gave him a seat and at night he lay with his feet to the fire.

The next morning the rabbit went to the lodge of the bear chief. They sat together awhile and smoked. At last the bear chief spoke.

"What do you want, my grandson?"

"I have come for some flint to make arrows," answered the rabbit.

The bear chief grunted, and laid aside his pipe. Leaning back, he pulled off his robe and, sure enough, one half of his body was flesh and the other half hard flint.

"Bring a stone hammer and give it to our guest," he bade his wife. Then as the rabbit took the hammer he said: "Do not strike too hard."

"Grandfather, I shall be careful," said the rabbit. With a stroke he struck off a little flake of flint from the bear's body.

"Ni-sko-ke-cha? So big?" he asked.

"Harder, grandson; strike off bigger pieces," said the bear.

The rabbit struck a little harder.

"Ni-sko-ke-cha? So big?" he asked.

The bear grew impatient. "No, no, strike off bigger pieces. I can't be here all day. Tanka kaksa wo! Break off a big piece."

The rabbit struck again -- hard! "Ni-sko -- cha?" he cried, as the hammer fell. But even as he spoke the bear's body broke in two, the flesh part fell away and only the flint part remained. Like a flash the rabbit darted out of the hut.

There was a great outcry in the village. Open-mouthed, all the bears gave chase. But as he ran the rabbit cried: "Wa-hin-han-yo (snow, snow) Ota-po, Ota-po -- lots more, lots more," and a great storm of snow swept down from the sky.

The rabbit, light of foot, bounded over the top of the snow. The bears sunk in and floundered about helpless. Seeing this, the rabbit turned back and killed them one by one with his club. That is why we now have so few bears.

About the Author

Thanks for choosing this book, if you enjoyed it, please leave positive feedback.

G.W. Mullins is an Author, Photographer, and Entrepreneur of Native American / Cherokee descent. He has been a published author for over 10 years. His writing has focused on the paranormal and Native American studies.

Mullins has released several books on the history/stories/fables of the Native American Indians. Among his books are the extremely successful "Star People, Sky Gods and Other Tales of the Native American Indians," "Story Teller An Anthology Of Folklore From The Native American Indians," "The Native American Story Book - Stories Of The American Indians For Children Volumes 1-5," "The Native American Cookbook," and "Walking With Spirits Native American Myths, Legends, And Folklore Volumes 1 Thru 6."

He has released the complete series of his Sci/fi Fantasy books "From The Dead Of Night," including the Best-Selling titles - Daniel Is Waiting, and Daniel Returns.

His most recent work includes the series Rise Of The Snow Queen featuring Book One The Polar Bear King and Book Two War Of The Witches. Mullins' latest releases include two young adult fantasy series, Rise of the Darklighter Book One Dark Awakening and

Dream Walker Book One Enter the Sandman. Among his other releases are Messages from The Other Side (a nonfiction book about communication with the dead), and the soon to be released “Convergence” (a post-apocalyptic book multi-series event coming in winter 2021).

For further information, on the writing, visit G.W. Mullins' web site at http://gwmullins.wix.com/books.

Also Available From G.W. Mullins

Daniel Awakens A Ghost Story Begins– From The Dead Of Night Prequel

Daniel Is Waiting A Ghost Story – From The Dead Of Night Book One

Daniel Returns A Ghost Story - From The Dead Of Night Book Two

Daniel's Fate – A Ghost Story Ends From The Dead Of Night Book Four

Rise Of The Snow Queen Book One The Polar Bear King

Messages From The Other Side Stories of the Dead, Their Communication, and Unfinished Business

Vengeance

Mysteries Of The Unseen World – Ghost, Hauntings and The Unexplained

Haunted America Stories Of Ghost, Hauntings And The Unexplained

Timeless A Paranormal Romance Murder Mystery

Star People, Sky Gods, And Other Tales Of The Native American Indians

Walking With Spirits Native American Myths, Legends, And Folklore Volumes One Thru Six

The Native American Cookbook

Native American Cooking - An Indian Cookbook With Legends And Folklore

Bear Tales Of The Native American Indians

The Native American Story Book - Stories Of The American Indians For Children Volumes One Thru Five

The Best Native American Stories For Children

Cherokee A Collection of American Indian Legends, Stories And Fables

Creation Myths - Tales Of The Native American Indians

Strange Tales Of The Native American Indians

Spirit Quest - Stories Of The Native American Indians

Animal Tales Of The Native American Indians

Medicine Man - Shamanism, Natural Healing, Remedies And Stories Of The Native American Indians

Native American Legends: Stories Of The Hopi Indians Volumes One and Two

Totem Animals Of The Native Americans

The Best Native American Myths, Legends And Folklore Volumes One Thru Three

Ghosts, Spirits And The Afterlife In Native American Indian Mythology And Folklore

War Song: Tales Of The Native American Indians

Origin Tales Of The Native American Indians

Animal Tales Of The Native American Indians Vol. 2

More Star People, Sky Gods, And Other Paranormal Tales Of The Native American Indians

www.ingramcontent.com/pod-product-compliance
Lightning Source LLC
Chambersburg PA
CBHW070353200726
48294CB00003B/891
9781737710073